I0118020

365 Writing Prompts

2020 Edition

Written by Jaz Johnson

Edited by Jaz Johnson & Brandon Tate

Formatted by Jaz Johnson

Cover Design by Jaz Johnson

First paperback edition published January 1st, 2020.

ISBN: 978-1-951626-10-5 (e-book)

ISBN: 978-1-951626-11-2 (paperback)

Published by TC Studios LLC

www.TCStudiosHQ.com

Table Of Contents

Introductions

Hello! Welcome to our 2020 edition of *365 Writing Prompts*. This book is a part of our creative group, **Prompt Party**. It's going to get your creative mojo flowing and make you want to start writing!

This book includes the following:

1. 365 prompts in ten different genres (a), and twelve different themes (b).
    a. Fantasy (F), Science Fiction (SF), Romance (R), Horror (H), Dystopian (D), Slice of Life (SL), Action & Adventure (AA), Mystery (M), Supernatural (S), and Paranormal (P).
    b. People, Time, Animals, Technology, Places, Science, Emotion, Food, Magic, Supernatural, Villains, and Words.
2. 73 writing exercises.

How To Use Our Prompts

Each prompt will list a hypothetical situation and a few suggested mediums to draw with, as well as suggested paths you can take with the prompt. You are **not** required to draw in with mediums or use the brainstorming sections. They are **only suggestions**.

Some prompts talk about you, but you don't always have to draw/write yourself. You can make up a character, or characters, too!

The goal is to draw or write a piece of work using the prompts provided. How you get there is ultimately up to you.

Share Your Work & Tag Us

We would love to be able to see the amazing things you come up with and tell you how much we love them.

To do that, all you have to do is post your work to Facebook, Instagram or Twitter and tag us @PromptParty. Then we'll be able to see, share, and comment on them!

Submit To Our Anthologies

Would you like your work to be published? People are using our prompt books across the country, and many of them are submitting their work to our annual anthologies.

An anthology is a collection of work by many different people. Each year, we publish several with work made using our various prompt books.

The authors of the published submissions receive 25% royalties (must be 18+), and 10% goes back into helping communities like yours. This money goes towards public school donations, public library donations, and more. So, help your community out by getting more people involved!

For more details on royalties and our mission to give back to communities across the country, visit our website, www.TCStudiosHQ.com.

To submit your work to our anthology, please do the following:

- Send an email to submissions@tcstudioshq.com with the following:
    - **Subject Line:**
        - 365 Writing Prompts Anthology Submission (2020)
    - **Body:**
        - First and last name (or pen/artist name).
        - The genre you used.
    - **Attachments:**
        - Attached work.
            - Attached as a **PDF** for literature.
        - Attached signed publication form.
            - You can find this on our website.

If you are selected, we will reach out to you to request more information.

For more information on our other anthologies and an in-depth guide on how to submit to them, visit our website, www.TCStuidiosHQ.com.

Chapter One: People.

#1 – You've discovered a long lost relative. (M) (SL) (S)

Brainstorm ...

- Is it your twin? Father? Ancestor that should have died hundreds of years ago but is somehow alive today? Your unborn child from the future?
  - How might who the relative is affect the story? How might it shape the story's background?
- How were they discovered?
  - Did you find them? Or did they find you?
  - Was it an accident? On purpose?
  - What happens now that you've found them?

You can share your work with us on Facebook, Instagram & Twitter!

Tag us @PromptParty and use #PromptParty.

We'd love to see what you come up with!

#2 – You run into yourself in a dream, but something isn't right – they're trying their hardest to stay away from you. (SF) (S) (AA)

Brainstorm …

- Why are they running from you?
    - What happens if you catch them?
    - How far are they willing to go to stay away from you?
- Where did you find them?
    - Is there anything you notice about the dream that might concern you?

Do you want your work published?

You can submit any work made using our prompts to our annual anthologies! Published submissions receive shared 25% royalties.

You can find more information on our website, www.TCStudiosHQ.com.

#3 – Someone has just broken into your home with malicious intent. (H) (SL) (AA)

Brainstorm …

- Is it a stranger, or someone you know?
    - Has someone been hired to kill you?
    - Are they merely there to steal?
    - Do they know you're home?
- Will you hide, or fight?
    - What would your strategy be?
    - Will you call the police? Try to escape?

Did you know?

A percentage of every anthology sold goes towards helping communities like yours. This includes donations to charities, funding of scholarships, creating of programs, and more!

You can find more information on our website, www.TCStudiosHQ.com.

#4 – You've just won a date with your favorite celebrity. They're picking you up tonight at 7PM. (R) (SL) (H)

Brainstorm …

- How do they feel about the date?
    - Are they excited? Upset? Annoyed? Nervous?
- Are they as you imagined?
    - Are they as perfect as you dreamed? Or are they an absolute nightmare?
- Are they married?
    - How does their spouse feel about the date?
- What did you have to do to win the date?
    - Do you regret it? Was it worth it?

Did you know?

In addition to our annual prompt anthologies, every year we have themed anthologies that you can also submit to!

You can find more information on our website, www.TCStudiosHQ.com.

#5 – "Where were you last night?" (M) (R) (SL)

Brainstorm ...

- Who are you speaking to?
    - Your lover? Child? Roommate?
- Why might they have been out so late? Why were you waiting up for them?
- What are you feeling?
    - Are you upset? Worried? Teasing?

Writing Exercise #1

Create three characters based on three of your favorite colors.

#6 – You can't keep your eyes off the new intern. (R) (SL) (M)

Brainstorm …

- Have they noticed?
    - Do they share your interest, or are you making them uncomfortable?
- Why are you watching them?
    - Do you want to ask them out?
    - Are they up to something bad?
    - Do you know them outside of work?
- Is anyone else watching?
    - Is there competition? Have you been given a warning?

Looking for a challenge?

Try writing about one of our prompts with your friend(s)! See if you can come up with something together.

#7 – You've been given a treasure map by a homeless man. (AA) (F) (M)

Brainstorm …

- Where is the treasure?
  - Is this a map of your state? Your country? Somewhere else?
- Can you read it?
  - Is the map in English?
  - If not, do you know someone who can help you translate it?
- Who is this man?
  - Who is he, and why is he now homeless?
  - Why is he entrusting the map to you?

Did you know?

We also make books to help with storytelling. With help on things like creating characters, world-building, magic systems, and more!

You can find more information on our website, www.TCStudiosHQ.com.

#8 – You've just found out that your best friend is an alien. (SF) (M) (H)

Brainstorm ...

- How long have you known them?
- How did you find out?
  - What is your reaction?
    - Are you surprised?
    - Are you offended?
    - Are you scared?
- Why were they keeping it a secret?
  - Do they have a different natural appearance?
  - Do they have a spaceship?
  - What else are they hiding?

Did you know?

We also publish novels and comics that you can read!

You can find more information on our website,
www.TCStudiosHQ.com.

#9 – You've been hired as a private investigator. (M) (S) (F)

Brainstorm ...

- What are you investigating?
- Who were you hired by?
- What are your methods?
    - Do you have any partners?
    - What is your workspace like?
    - How quickly can you get results?

Do you want to give us a prompt for next year's edition?

You can submit prompt ideas you have based on next year's chapter themes. Credit will be given if selected.

You can find more information on our website, www.TCStudiosHQ.com.

#10 – You are given the opportunity to meet the person that has given you one of their kidneys. (SL) (P) (H)

> **Brainstorm ...**
>
> - What would you say to them?
> - How has your health been since receiving the kidney?
> - How long had you been waiting for it?
>   - What was your life like before getting it?

Writing Exercise #2

Write about a new-found love with someone.

#11 – You are watching your loved one turn into a zombie. (H) (P) (D)

Brainstorm …

- How did it happen?
  - Were they bitten?
    - Where? How many times?
  - Did they just die?
  - Were they infected some other way?
- What is your reaction?
  - Do you have it in you to kill them?
    - How do you say your farewell?
  - Will you run away?
  - Will you end up getting bitten as well?

Did you know?

We post daily writing & drawing prompts on our Social Medias for everyone to participate in.

Find us @PromptParty and use #PromptParty.

You can find more information on our website, www.TCStudiosHQ.com.

#12 – You receive a letter from your ex-fiancé. (R) (M) (SL)

Brainstorm ...

- What could it say?
  - Are they apologizing?
  - Are they after your new-found riches?
  - Has a child in their custody fallen ill?
  - Are they in trouble?

Did you know?

In addition to posting daily on Social Media, we have daily interactive posts on our YouTube channel, Podcast, and Blog.

You can find more information on our website, www.TCStudiosHQ.com.

#13 – Someone picks you up hitchhiking. (H) (R) (M)

Brainstorm …

- Were you asking, or was it random?
- What kind of vehicle are they driving?
- What does the person look like?
    - Are they alone?
- Where are they headed?
    - Where are you headed?
- Do you end up regretting the decision? Are you happy about it?

Remember!

The listed genres/mediums and brainstorming boxes are **only suggestions!** We encourage you to do/use whatever you want.

#14 – "Don't you dare." (SL) (P) (S)

Brainstorm …

- Are you saying this, or is it being said to you?
- What are either of you about to do?
    - What happens if you do?
    - What happens if you don't?
    - Are there consequences?
        - Good?
        - Bad?
        - For who?

Be The First To Know.

Join our newsletter and be the first to know about new prompt books, novels, comics, giveaways, freebies, coupons, and anything else we've got going on!

Find our newsletter on our website, www.TCStudiosHQ.com.

#15 – People are cheering your name. (SL) (AA) (D)

> ### *Brainstorm …*
>
> - Are you a hero?
> - Have you done something heroic?
>   - What might that be?
>   - What did it take for you to do it?
>   - Are you in the process of doing it?
>   - Are you in danger of not completing it?
>   - Are they trying to give you strength?
>   - Have you completed your task?
>   - What happens now?

Writing Exercise #3

Write about someone being betrayed by their best friend.

#16 – You're a pirate preparing to set sail. (F) (AA) (S)

Brainstorm …

- Where are you currently docked?
  - Why did you dock?
    - Were you out of food?
    - Were you docking to trade or hide your bounty?
- Where are you headed now?
- Who makes up your crew?
- Are you well-prepared?
  - Are you leaving in a hurry?
    - Is someone after you?

You can share your work with us on Facebook, Instagram & Twitter!

Tag us @PromptParty and use #PromptParty.

We'd love to see what you come up with!

#17 – There's a ghost living in your attic. (H) (P) (S)

Brainstorm …

- Has it always been there or is this a new encounter?
    - If it's new, what changed to bring the ghost?
- Is the ghost friendly or hostile?
- Do you want to get rid of it?
    - How would you do that?
- Do you want to help it?
    - How would you do that?

Do you want your work published?

You can submit any work made using our prompts to our annual anthologies! Published submissions receive shared 25% royalties.

You can find more information on our website, www.TCStudiosHQ.com.

#18 – You're about to meet an author who has changed your life. (SL) (SF) (R)

Brainstorm ...

- What would you say to them?
- Would you ask for an autograph? A picture?
- Would you bring them a gift?
- How did they change your life?

Did you know?

A percentage of every anthology sold goes towards helping communities like yours. This includes donations to charities, funding of scholarships, creating of programs, and more!

You can find more information on our website, www.TCStudiosHQ.com.

#19 – You find someone sitting on your porch. (SL) (M) (R)

Brainstorm ...

- What are they doing?
- How long have they been there?
- Why are they there?
    - Are they there to see you?
    - Are they resting from traveling?
    - Are they looking for someone else?
- Are they friendly? Dangerous?

Did you know?

In addition to our annual prompt anthologies, every year we have <u>themed</u> anthologies that you can also submit to!

You can find more information on our website,
www.TCStudiosHQ.com.

#20 – Someone's child is lost in the park. (SL) (M) (H)

Brainstorm ...

- Where is their parent/guardian?
  - o Did something happen to them?
  - o Have they abandoned the child?
- What is the child doing?
  - o Are they looking for someone?
  - o Are they crying?
  - o Are they carefree?
- What will you do about it?
  - o Take them to the police?
  - o Help them find their parent/guardian?

Writing Exercise #4

Create a character based on what you had for breakfast.

#21 – "What have you done?" (SL) (D) (P)

Brainstorm …

- How is this question being asked?
  - In horror?
  - In calm curiosity?
- What's going to happen now that it's been done?
- Can it be undone?

Looking for a challenge?

Try writing about one of our prompts with your friend(s)! See if you can come up with something together.

#22 – Your best friend's lover has just confessed their love for you. (R) (SL) (M)

Brainstorm …

- How did they do it?
  - Suddenly?
  - Did they plan it around your friend's absence?
- How do you feel about it?
  - Are you deathly uncomfortable?
  - Have you secretly wanted to be with them?
  - Will you tell your friend?

Did you know?

We also make books to help with storytelling. With help on things like creating characters, world-building, magic systems, and more!

You can find more information on our website,
www.TCStudiosHQ.com.

#23 – You're having a family reunion. (SL) (H) (AA)

Brainstorm …

- Do you want to go?
  - o   Are you reluctant?
- Is there anyone you're excited to see?
  - o   Anyone you hope isn't there?
- Is there any drama or tension in the family?
- Why is there a reunion happening?

Did you know?

We also publish novels and comics that you can read!

You can find more information on our website,
www.TCStudiosHQ.com.

#24 – A loved one is brought back to life – for a price. (H) (P) (S)

Brainstorm ...

- Who is brought back?
  - How do they feel about it?
  - What did it cost?
- How will your lives be different now that they're back?
  - Do you have to hide them?
  - Do you have to change their appearance?
  - Are there any physical problems with coming back from the dead?

Do you want to give us a prompt for next year's edition?

You can submit prompt ideas you have based on next year's chapter themes. Credit will be given if selected.

You can find more information on our website, www.TCStudiosHQ.com.

#25 – A killer is on the loose in your town. (H) (M) (AA)

Brainstorm …

- How many people have they killed?
    - Did you know any of them?
- Why are they killing them?
    - Is it targeted or at random?
    - Are the people innocent or criminal?
- Is there anything you can do about it?
    - What are the police doing about it?

Writing Exercise #5

Write about a fight between two people.

#26 – You're at the wrong place at the wrong time. (SL) (AA) (H)

Brainstorm ...

- What and who have you just seen?
    - A murder?
    - A robbery?
- What does it mean for you?
    - Did they see you?
        - Are you in danger?
        - Did you accidently get involved?

Did you know?

We post daily writing & drawing prompts on our Social Medias for everyone to participate in.

Find us @PromptParty and use #PromptParty.

You can find more information on our website, www.TCStudiosHQ.com.

#27 – You just discovered you have extraordinary powers. (F) (SF) (S)

Brainstorm ...

- What are they?
    - What can they do?
    - Do they have limits?
    - Do they have requirements?
- What do you plan on doing with them?
    - Mundane things?
    - Heroic things?
    - Keep them a secret?
    - Tell others?

Did you know?

In addition to posting daily on Social Media, we have daily interactive posts on our YouTube channel, Podcast, and Blog.

You can find more information on our website, www.TCStudiosHQ.com.

#28 – You're being hunted down. (H) (AA) (S)

Brainstorm ...

- By what or whom?
- Why?
- How long have they been after you?
    - How far have they traveled in the process?
    - What have you done to stay out of their grasp?
- What can you do to stop the hunt?
    - What do they want from you?

Remember!

The listed genres/mediums and brainstorming boxes are **only suggestions!** We encourage you to do/use whatever you want.

#29 – You're one of the last humans to survive. (D) (M) (S)

Brainstorm ...

- To survive what?
    - The end of the world?
    - A war?
    - A natural disaster?
    - An alien invasion?
- How did you survive?
    - Why didn't others?
- What will you do now?
    - How will you survive?
    - Will you look for others to be sure you're not alone?

Be The First To Know.

Join our newsletter and be the first to know about new prompt books, novels, comics, giveaways, freebies, coupons, and anything else we've got going on!

Find our newsletter on our website, www.TCStudiosHQ.com.

#30 – "You'll pay for this!" (AA) (SL) (SF)

Brainstorm …

- Is this being said figuratively or literally?
    - Do you have the means to pay for whatever it is financially?
    - Would you have to pay with your life?
- What are you paying for?
    - What did you do?
    - Who did you do it to?

Writing Exercise #6

Write about meeting someone for the first time.

#31 – You regret your decision. (SL) (SF) (D)

> ***Brainstorm …***
>
> - What did you decide to do?
>   - How is it affecting your life?
>   - How is it affecting other people's lives?
>   - Was there a better decision to be made?
>   - Did someone try to warn you beforehand?

You can share your work with us on Facebook, Instagram & Twitter!

Tag us @PromptParty and use #PromptParty.

We'd love to see what you come up with!

Chapter Two: Time.

#32 – You're running out of time. (SL) (H) (AA)

Brainstorm ...

- Running out of time to do what?
    - o Do something?
    - o Go somewhere?
    - o Live?
- What happens if time runs out?
    - o How will you make sure it doesn't?
    - o What will you do if it does?

Do you want your work published?

You can submit any work made using our prompts to our annual anthologies! Published submissions receive shared 25% royalties.

You can find more information on our website, www.TCStudiosHQ.com.

#33 – There's a ticking time-bomb. Red wire, or blue? (AA) (SF) (M)

Brainstorm ...

- Do you have any training to disarm bombs?
    - If not, is there enough time to get someone who is?
- Where did the bomb come from?
    - Why has it been set?
    - Where has it been placed?
    - Who is in danger if it explodes?
    - Is it a fake/dud?
- How did you find yourself in this situation?
- Is there another way to get rid of the bomb?

Did you know?

A percentage of every anthology sold goes towards helping communities like yours. This includes donations to charities, funding of scholarships, creating of programs, and more!

You can find more information on our website, www.TCStudiosHQ.com.

#34 – You wake up 100 years in the future. (SF) (M) (AA)

Brainstorm …

- How did you get there?
    - Have you been cursed?
    - Were you frozen?
    - Were you transported?
- What is the future like?
    - Where did you wake up?
    - Is there anyone you know?
- Do you want to go back to the present?
    - How would you do that?
    - Is this where you need to be?

Did you know?

In addition to our annual prompt anthologies, every year we have themed anthologies that you can also submit to!

You can find more information on our website, www.TCStudiosHQ.com.

#35 – You wake up 100 years in the past. (SF) (M) (AA)

Brainstorm …

- How did you get there?
    - Have you been cursed?
    - Were you frozen?
    - Were you transported?
- What is the past like?
    - Where did you wake up?
    - Is there anyone you know?
- Do you want to go back to the present?
    - How would you do that?
    - Is this where you need to be?

Writing Exercise #7

Write about someone who is running late for something.

#36 – You've got a blind date at 8PM. (M) (R) (SL)

Brainstorm …

- Did you arrange this or did someone else?
  - Was it through a dating site/app?
  - Did a friend set you up?
- How do you feel about the date?
  - Are you looking forward to it?
  - Are you dreading it?
- How are you preparing for the date?
  - Are you fussing over how you look?
  - Are you planning on flaking?

Looking for a challenge?

Try writing about one of our prompts with your friend(s)! See if you can come up with something together.

#37 – "Any second now." (AA) (SL) (F)

Brainstorm …

- What's about to happen?
    - Are you waiting for a ride?
    - Is someone about to give you the signal?
    - Is your food about to be delivered?
- How do you feel about waiting?
    - Are you excited?
    - Are you impatient?
    - Are you anxious?
- What happens if it never comes?
    - What happens when it does?

Did you know?

We also make books to help with storytelling. With help on things like creating characters, world-building, magic systems, and more!

You can find more information on our website,
www.TCStudiosHQ.com.

#38 – "We don't have time for this!" (AA) (SL) (S)

Brainstorm …

- Why?
  - Is something going to happen soon?
  - Is someone just impatient?
- What is it that they don't have time for?

Did you know?

We also publish novels and comics that you can read!

You can find more information on our website,
www.TCStudiosHQ.com.

#39 – "You've got ten seconds." (AA) (SL) (H)

Brainstorm …

- To do what?
    - What happens once you do it?
    - What happens if you don't?
- Until what?
    - What's about to happen?
    - Who or what is behind it?
    - Are you trying to stop it?
    - Do you want it to happen?

Do you want to give us a prompt for next year's edition?

You can submit prompt ideas you have based on next year's chapter themes. Credit will be given if selected.

You can find more information on our website,
www.TCStudiosHQ.com.

#40 – "When?" (SL) (M) (R)

Brainstorm …

- What is being asked about?
  - Why is the time important?
  - Will it clash with a different schedule?
  - Are they talking about the day or time?

Writing Exercise #8

Write about someone who is tired of waiting.

#41 – It's 2AM and you can't sleep. (SL) (H) (P)

Brainstorm ...

- Why?
    - Too much caffeine?
    - Insomnia?
    - Nightmares?
    - Late night thoughts?
- What are you going to do since you can't sleep?
    - Jog?
    - Read?
    - Watch a show?

Did you know?

We post daily writing & drawing prompts on our Social Medias for everyone to participate in.

Find us @PromptParty and use #PromptParty.

You can find more information on our website, www.TCStudiosHQ.com.

#42 – The only way to save the future is to destroy the past. (SF) (AA) (S)

Brainstorm ...

- What does this mean?
  - ○ Is it literal or figurative?
  - ○ Are they going to destroy books?
  - ○ Go back in time and change history?
- Think about the different ways this could be used in context.

Did you know?

In addition to posting daily on Social Media, we have daily interactive posts on our YouTube channel, Podcast, and Blog.

You can find more information on our website, www.TCStudiosHQ.com.

#43 – You're tired of waiting. It's time to take action. (AA) (SL) (F)

Brainstorm ...

- What were you waiting around for?
    - For someone else to step up?
    - For something to pass?
    - For something to happen?
- What does taking action mean in this situation?
    - Rescuing people?
    - Putting out a fire?
    - Starting a mission?

Remember!

The listed genres/mediums and brainstorming boxes are **only suggestions!** We encourage you to do/use whatever you want.

#44 – You've got one minute to sever your arm, or you'll die. (H) (AA) (SF)

Brainstorm …

- What could be the reason behind this?
  - Is your arm stuck in something?
    - Is something about to kill you because of it?
- How are you going to do it?
  - What's around you that you can use?
- Are you going to choose death?
  - How would you die?

Be The First To Know.

Join our newsletter and be the first to know about new prompt books, novels, comics, giveaways, freebies, coupons, and anything else we've got going on!

Find our newsletter on our website, www.TCStudiosHQ.com.

#45 – All of the clocks in your home have stopped. (M) (P) (SF)

Brainstorm ...

- Why?
  - ○ Was there a power surge? An EMP?
  - ○ Is your home haunted?
    - ▪ Is the ghost mad?
- What are you going to do about it?

Writing Exercise #9

Write about a world with 30 hours in the day.

#46 – It starts at midnight. Hope you're ready. (AA) (F) (D)

Brainstorm …

- What starts?
    - Is it exciting?
    - Is it dangerous?
    - Is it romantic?
- What do you need to do to prepare for it?
- Do you plan on participating?
    - Do you have a choice?

You can share your work with us on Facebook, Instagram & Twitter!

Tag us @PromptParty and use #PromptParty.

We'd love to see what you come up with!

#47 – "What a time to be alive." (SL) (SF) (D)

Brainstorm ...

- What's going on that they would say this?
  - Something good?
  - Something bad?
  - Is there a revolution happening?
  - A surge of new technology?
- What does this "time" mean for them?
  - Are they positively or negatively affected?

Do you want your work published?

You can submit any work made using our prompts to our annual anthologies! Published submissions receive shared 25% royalties.

You can find more information on our website, www.TCStudiosHQ.com.

#48 – Your spell will only last for two minutes. (F) (S) (AA)

Brainstorm ...

- What kind of spell is it?
  - What does it do?
- Is two minutes enough time?
  - What happens if it's not?
  - What happens if it is?
  - Who/what will be affected by the outcome?
- Who is casting the spell?
- What/who is it being directed at?

Did you know?

A percentage of every anthology sold goes towards helping communities like yours. This includes donations to charities, funding of scholarships, creating of programs, and more!

You can find more information on our website, www.TCStudiosHQ.com.

#49 – "Get here by noon, or she dies." (M) (SL) (D)

Brainstorm …

- Get where?
- Who has been taken?
  - By whom?
  - Is it more than one person behind this?
  - What do they want?
    - From whom?
- What is this person going to do?
  - Will they bring backup?
  - Will they call the police?
  - Is the person making threats setting any specific terms?

Did you know?

In addition to our annual prompt anthologies, every year we have themed anthologies that you can also submit to!

You can find more information on our website, www.TCStudiosHQ.com.

#50 – "Good timing." (SL) (SF) (S)

Brainstorm ...

- What is?
    - What just happened?
    - What would have happened if it was bad timing?
- Who or what is involved?

Writing Exercise #10

Write about someone who wants to make up for lost time.

#51 – If you had the ability to see your future, would you? (SF) (S) (M)

Brainstorm …

- How might you have acquired the ability to do that?
    - A machine?
    - A wizard?
    - A fortune teller?
        - Would there be any conditions?
- What would you do if it was negative?
    - What would happen if you tried to change it?
- What would you do if it was positive?

Looking for a challenge?

Try writing about one of our prompts with your friend(s)! See if you can come up with something together.

#52 – If you could change one thing from your past, what would it be? (SF) (SL) (R)

> ### *Brainstorm …*
>
> - Why would you change what you chose?
>   - How do you think it would affect your present?
> - What if there was a way you could?
>   - How would you?
>   - Would it cost anything?

Did you know?

We also make books to help with storytelling. With help on things like creating characters, world-building, magic systems, and more!

You can find more information on our website,
www.TCStudiosHQ.com.

#53 – The ability to stop time. (F) (S) (SF)

Brainstorm …

- Do you have it?
- Does someone else?
- Does something else?
- What would it be used for?
    - To stop crime?
    - To change the outcome of something?
    - Would there be consequences

Did you know?

We also publish novels and comics that you can read!

You can find more information on our website,
www.TCStudiosHQ.com.

#54 – You have a time-based OCD. (SL) (SF) (M)

> **Brainstorm …**
>
> - How does this affect your life?
> - What changes would you be making in your life to accommodate it?
> - Would it positively or negatively impact you?
> - Are you trying to overcome it?
>   - How are you going about doing that?
>   - Is anyone trying to help?
> - How are other people affected by the OCD?

Do you want to give us a prompt for next year's edition?

You can submit prompt ideas you have based on next year's chapter themes. Credit will be given if selected.

You can find more information on our website, www.TCStudiosHQ.com.

#55 – You're immortal. (S) (SF) (R)

Brainstorm ...

- What do you do with all your time?
    - What have you been doing?
    - What have you accomplished?
- Do you know any other immortals?
- Do you interact with mortals?
- Are you tired of living?
    - Have you tried to die?
    - Is there a way that you can?
- How did you become immortal?
    - Were you born that way?
    - Did something happen?

Writing Exercise #11

Write about someone who is a stickler for being on time.

60

#56 – "There's no time! Go!" (AA) (F) (D)

Brainstorm ...

- No time for what?
- What is someone trying to do?
  - o Why don't they have time?
- What happens if they run out of time, or are late?
- What are they willing to do to stay on time?
- Where are they going?
  - o Why do they need to go?
  - o What did they need to do?

Did you know?

We post daily writing & drawing prompts on our Social Medias for everyone to participate in.

Find us @PromptParty and use #PromptParty.

You can find more information on our website, www.TCStudiosHQ.com.

#57 – The dragons soar through the skies every night at dusk. (F) (SL) (R)

Brainstorm …

- Where are they being seen from?
- Are the people watching scared of them?
- Are they hiding from them?
  - Do they stay hidden at dusk?
- Is anyone friendly with the dragons?
  - Do they fly with them?

Remember!

The listed genres/mediums and brainstorming boxes are **only suggestions!** We encourage you to do/use whatever you want.

\#58 – Everything's happening in slow motion. (S) (SF) (M)

Brainstorm …

- Why?
  - Have you been drugged?
  - Are you hallucinating?
  - Are you moving super-fast?
- When will it stop?
  - Will it?
- Are you the only one that can see it?

You can share your work with us on Facebook, Instagram & Twitter!

Tag us @PromptParty and use #PromptParty.

We'd love to see what you come up with!

#59– You find a pocket watch. Engraved on the back reads "Now it's your turn". (AA) (R) (SF)

Brainstorm ...

- Where did you find it?
- Is there anyone around?
- Is the watch working?
  - What condition is it in?
- What material is it made of?
- What are you going to do now?

Do you want your work published?

You can submit any work made using our prompts to our annual anthologies! Published submissions receive shared 25% royalties.

You can find more information on our website,
www.TCStudiosHQ.com.

#60 – You're face to face with Father Time. (F) (S) (AA)

Brainstorm …

- How did you get there?
  - Where are you?
- What does he look like?
- Why are you there?
  - What will you talk about?
  - Is something wrong with time?
  - Has he summoned you or have you summoned him?

Writing Exercise #12

Write about someone who is out of time.

Chapter Three: Animals.

#61 – Cats with opposable thumbs. (S) (H) (D)

Brainstorm …

- Why?
- How?
- How could this change their hierarchy?
- What are they doing with their thumbs?
    - Have they learned to use tools?
- Is this a new mutation or a different species?
- Is this from experimenting?

Did you know?

A percentage of every anthology sold goes towards helping communities like yours. This includes donations to charities, funding of scholarships, creating of programs, and more!

You can find more information on our website, www.TCStudiosHQ.com.

#62 – The ability to speak to and understand animals. (F) (S) (SF)

Brainstorm ...

- What might be some things that they say?
- What are some things you'd say to them?
- Would you act as a translator for humans and their pets?
- Would you advocate for stopping animal cruelty?
- What might be some side effects of this ability?
  - Are they negative?
  - Are they positive?

Did you know?

In addition to our annual prompt anthologies, every year we have themed anthologies that you can also submit to!

You can find more information on our website, www.TCStudiosHQ.com.

#63 – You are a crossbreed between a human and a mystical creature. (F) (SF) (S)

Brainstorm ...

- Which mystical creature?
    - What features does this give you as a result?
- Are you accepted by either side of your family?
- Do you know any other crossbreeds?
- What is your speech like?
- How did your parents end up together?
    - Are they still together?
    - Were they ever?

Looking for a challenge?

Try doing one of our prompts with your friend(s)! See if you can come up with something together.

#64 – Flying monkeys! (S) (H) (SL)

Brainstorm ...

- Where?
- Why?
- What are they doing?
- Are they docile or aggressive?
- Where did they come from?
- What else can they do?

Did you know?

We also make books to help with storytelling. With help on things like creating characters, world-building, magic systems, and more!

You can find more information on our website,
www.TCStudiosHQ.com.

#65 – A dinosaur egg just hatched at your local museum. (SF) (H) (AA)

Brainstorm …

- What kind of dinosaur?
    - ○ Carnivore? Herbivore?
- Was the hatching an accident or on purpose?
- What are they going to do with it?
    - ○ Who will keep it?
    - ○ Where will it live?
    - ○ Will the government allow it?

Writing Exercise #13

Write about the adventures of a lost pet.

#66 – You're a dragon tamer. (F) (AA) (D)

Brainstorm ...

- What kind of dragons do you tame?
    - o Is there a specific element, or are you well-rounded?
- Can you speak to them?
    - o Can they speak to you?
- What do you do with them?
    - o Do they help you with tasks?
    - o Are they friendly towards other people?
- How long have you been taming dragons?
    - o How do you do it?

Did you know?

We also publish novels and comics that you can read!

You can find more information on our website,
www.TCStudiosHQ.com.

#67 – Down the rabbit hole we go. (AA) (SF) (P)

Brainstorm …

- Is this figurative or literal?
- What's down the rabbit hole, in either sense?
  - Is it good or bad?
  - Did you want to go down the rabbit hole?
    - Why or why not?

Do you want to give us a prompt for next year's edition?

You can submit prompt ideas you have based on next year's chapter themes. Credit will be given if selected.

You can find more information on our website, www.TCStudiosHQ.com.

#68 – "You dog, you." (SL) (R) (M)

Brainstorm ...

- What did this person do to warrant the comment?
- Is this person some sort of dog hybrid?
- Who is saying the comment?
- How do the people feel about said comment?

Did you know?

We post daily writing & drawing prompts on our Social Medias for everyone to participate in.

Find us @PromptParty and use #PromptParty.

You can find more information on our website, www.TCStudiosHQ.com.

#69 – "Yeah, when pigs fly." (SL) (H) (S)

Brainstorm …

- What is the context of this?
- Is someone skeptical about something?
- Is this being said literally?
    - Are there pigs that fly, and something that hinges on them flying?

Did you know?

In addition to posting daily on Social Media, we have daily interactive posts on our YouTube channel, Podcast, and Blog.

You can find more information on our website, www.TCStudiosHQ.com.

#70 – You've discovered a new species. (SF) (H) (SL)

Brainstorm …

- What kind?
    - Does it live in the water?
    - Can it fly?
    - Is it a mammal?
    - Is it nocturnal?
- Where was it discovered?
- Is there just one or were there many of them?
- Were you looking for it or was this a surprise?
- Where does it rank on the food chain?
    - Is it docile or aggressive?
- What will you do now?

Writing Exercise #14

Write about the world through the perspective of an animal.

75

#71 – You've just gotten a dog – only, it's not a dog. (SF) (H) (S)

Brainstorm ...

- What is it?
    - Another known species or something unknown?
- Where did you get it?
    - On the street?
    - In a shop?
        - Did they know it wasn't a dog?
- What will you do with it now?
- Is it dangerous? Friendly?
- What does it look like?
    - Does it have any odd/interesting features?

Remember!

The listed genres/mediums and brainstorming boxes are **only suggestions!** We encourage you to do/use whatever you want.

#72 – There's something growling out there in the darkness. (SL) (F) (AA)

Brainstorm ...

- Where are you?
  - Inside?
    - House?
    - Store?
  - Outside?
    - Cave?
    - Tent?
    - Woods?
- What could it be?
- Are you afraid?
- Are you prepared to fight it?
  - With what?
  - With who?

Be The First To Know.

Join our newsletter and be the first to know about new prompt books, novels, comics, giveaways, freebies, coupons, and anything else we've got going on!

Find our newsletter on our website, www.TCStudiosHQ.com.

#73 – Search hounds are hunting you down. (AA) (M) (D)

Brainstorm …

- Why?
    - What did you do?
    - Are you in danger?
    - Are people trying to save you or capture you?
- Where are you?
- Who sent the hounds?
- Do you want to be found?
    - Are you running away?

You can share your work with us on Facebook, Instagram & Twitter!

Tag us @PromptParty and use #PromptParty.

We'd love to see what you come up with!

\#74 – An animal that can speak English. (SF) (F) (S)

Brainstorm ...

- What kind of animal?
- How did they learn English?
- Where is it?
- Is it openly communicating with people or hiding from them?
- How was it discovered to know English?
- Does it use this ability for any kind of mayhem?

Do you want your work published?

You can submit any work made using our prompts to our annual anthologies! Published submissions receive shared 25% royalties.

You can find more information on our website,
www.TCStudiosHQ.com.

#75 – You've been transformed into an animal. (SF) (S) (SL)

Brainstorm …

- What kind of animal?
    - Are you in a suitable environment for it?
- What are your first actions like?
    - What is it like to be in this new body?
    - Are you panicking? Are you confused?
- How were you transformed?
- How would you go about be turned back?

Writing Exercise #15

Write about finding and taking in a baby animal.

#76 – You've found out your lover is a shapeshifter. (R) (S) (M)

Brainstorm …

- What do they turn into?
  - Are there conditions for them turning into it?
- Were they hiding it from you?
  - For how long?
  - Why?
- What are your thoughts now that you know?
  - Are you afraid?
  - Are you angry?
  - What are you going to do now?
    - Will you stay with them?
    - Will you run away?
      - Will they let you?

Did you know?

A percentage of every anthology sold goes towards helping communities like yours. This includes donations to charities, funding of scholarships, creating of programs, and more!

You can find more information on our website, www.TCStudiosHQ.com.

#77 – Animal control has just been called to your job.

Brainstorm ...

- Why?
- What animal is there?
  - How big is it?
  - Has it attacked anyone?
  - Is it causing property damage?
- How long will it take to get there?
  - Have people been evacuated?
- Where is the animal now?

Be The First To Know.

Join our newsletter and be the first to know about new prompt books, novels, comics, giveaways, freebies, coupons, and anything else we've got going on!

Find our newsletter on our website, www.TCStudiosHQ.com.

#78 – "Get that thing out of here!" (AA) (S) (P)

Brainstorm …

- What thing?
- Out of where?
- What is it doing?
    - Is it a threat to someone or something?
    - Is it scared and hiding?
- Is this person trying to protect someone or something?
    - Are they just not an animal person?
- Think about the context of this situation.

Did you know?

In addition to our annual prompt anthologies, every year we have
themed anthologies that you can also submit to!

You can find more information on our website,
www.TCStudiosHQ.com.

#79 – Animals are escaping from your local zoo. (AA) (SL) (M)

Brainstorm …

- How?
    - Are they breaking out of their exhibits?
    - Is someone letting them out?
- What are they doing now that they're out?
- How are they going to be put back in?
    - What is the zoo doing about it?
- When it this happening?
    - Day or night?
    - Is anyone around to stop it?

Looking for a challenge?

Try doing one of our prompts with your friend(s)! See if you can come up with something together.

#80 – You are face to face with a wary wildcat. (AA) (SL) (H)

Brainstorm ...

- Where are you?
  - o Are you in its habitat?
  - o Is it in yours?
- Does it look docile or aggressive?
- What wildcat is it?
- What was it doing in the area?
- What were you doing in the area?
- How are you going to get away?

Writing Exercise #16

Write about someone living in the wild.

85

#81 – An animal has come back from extinction. (SF) (H) (S)

Brainstorm ...

- Which one?
    - Where is it on the hierarchy?
    - What does this mean for humans?
    - What does this mean for animals?
- Where is this animal living?
- Who rediscovered it?
    - How?
- Will it be allowed to live?

Did you know?

We also make books to help with storytelling. With help on things like creating characters, world-building, magic systems, and more!

You can find more information on our website, www.TCStudiosHQ.com.

#82 – You've found a creature frozen in the tundra of Antarctica. (SF) (M) (AA)

Brainstorm ...

- What are you doing there?
  - Who are you with?
- What does the creature look like?
- How big is it?
- What features does it have?
- Are you going to try to get it out?
  - Thaw it?
  - Take it back with you?

Did you know?

We also publish novels and comics that you can read!

You can find more information on our website, www.TCStudiosHQ.com.

#83 – You've found a creature lurking in the depths of the ocean. (SF) (H) (AA)

Brainstorm …

- What are you doing out in the ocean?
- Were you looking for this creature?
  - Were there stories around it?
- What does it look like?
- How big is it?
- What features does it have?

Do you want to give us a prompt for next year's edition?

You can submit prompt ideas you have based on next year's chapter themes. Credit will be given if selected.

You can find more information on our website, www.TCStudiosHQ.com.

#84 – There's something aboard your ship – and it's hungry. (H) (M) (F)

Brainstorm …

- Where is it on the ship?
- Does anyone know it's there?
- How did it get there?
- Is it stealing food?
    - Is it eating people?
- How are you going to deal with it?
    - Will you escape?
    - Call the coast guard?
    - Try to kill it?

Did you know?

We post daily writing & drawing prompts on our Social Medias for everyone to participate in.

Find us @PromptParty and use #PromptParty.

You can find more information on our website, www.TCStudiosHQ.com.

#85 – A world run by animals. (SF) (D) (SL)

Brainstorm …

- When did it start?
  - o   Is it on Earth?
  - o   Is it from an experiment?
- Did you land on a planet where animals are in control?
- What is their society like?
- Are humans their pets?
  - o   Their comrades?

Writing Exercise #17

Write a short essay about your favorite animal.

#86 – All animals have begun to mysteriously die off. (M) (SF) (D)

Brainstorm ...

- Is anyone working to figure out why or how?
    - How are they going about doing that?
    - Who is working on it?
        - Are you involved?
    - Are they trying to save them?
        - How?

Did you know?

In addition to posting daily on Social Media, we have daily interactive posts on our YouTube channel, Podcast, and Blog.

You can find more information on our website, www.TCStudiosHQ.com.

#87 – A fishing trip gone wrong. (AA) (SL) (H)

Brainstorm …

- How so?
  - Did you forget something important?
  - Did you catch something dangerous' attention?
  - Did the boat get turned over?
  - Did you find a dangerous sea creature?
  - Did you run into pirates?

Remember!

The listed genres/mediums and brainstorming boxes are **only suggestions!** We encourage you to do/use whatever you want.

#88 – The oceans are being poisoned. (SL) (M) (AA)

Brainstorm ...

- By what?
- By whom?
- How fast is it spreading?
- How many animals is it killing?
- Is it contaminating anything else?
- How can it be stopped and cleaned?

Be The First To Know.

Join our newsletter and be the first to know about new prompt books, novels, comics, giveaways, freebies, coupons, and anything else we've got going on!

Find our newsletter on our website, www.TCStudiosHQ.com.

#89 – The spirit of a lost pet lingers around your house. (P) (S) (SL)

Brainstorm ...

- What is it doing?
- What animal is it?
- Is it docile or hostile?
- What does it want?
- Do you interact with it?
- Does in interact with anyone else?
    - Other animals?

You can share your work with us on Facebook, Instagram & Twitter!

Tag us @PromptParty and use #PromptParty.

We'd love to see what you come up with!

#90 – You do some bird calls in the woods - and something else answers. (H) (AA) (M)

> **Brainstorm …**
>
> - What were you originally hoping to find?
> - What answered instead?
>   - A person?
>   - A creature?
>   - What do they look like?
>   - Are they docile or hostile?
> - What will you do now?

Writing Exercise #18

Write about what it would be like if dinosaurs were alive today.

#91 – You find a wild horse nursing a unicorn. (F) (S) (M)

Brainstorm ...

- Where?
- Do they see you?
    - Are they spooked or remaining calm?
- Do you have a camera on you?
    - Will you take a picture?
    - Will you keep this moment to yourself?
- Are you able to get closer?

Do you want your work published?

You can submit any work made using our prompts to our annual anthologies! Published submissions receive shared 25% royalties.

You can find more information on our website, www.TCStudiosHQ.com.

Chapter Four: Technology.

#92 – The AI in your phone is trying to warn you. (SF) (M) (H)

Brainstorm …

- About what?
- How?
    - Is it speaking?
    - Is it typing?
    - Is it playing a song?
    - Is it ringing an alarm?
    - Is it being controlled/ordered by someone?
- Are you going to listen?
- How else can it help you?

Did you know?

A percentage of every anthology sold goes towards helping communities like yours. This includes donations to charities, funding of scholarships, creating of programs, and more!

You can find more information on our website, www.TCStudiosHQ.com.

#93 – Your car has taken over and is taking you somewhere. (SF) (AA) (S)

Brainstorm ...

- When did it start?
- Are the doors locked?
- Is there a GPS?
    - Is it showing where it's taking you?
- How fast is it going?
- Do you know where you are?
- Is there any way to stop it?
- Is there anyone with you?
- Is the car speaking?
    - Is it the car or someone communicating through it?

Did you know?

In addition to our annual prompt anthologies, every year we have themed anthologies that you can also submit to!

You can find more information on our website, www.TCStudiosHQ.com.

#94 – You've fallen in love with an AI. (R) (SF) (SL)

Brainstorm ...

- How long have you been interacting with it?
- What form does it take?
  - Humanoid?
  - A machine?
  - A device?
- Does anyone know?
  - If yes, how do they feel about it?
- Will you start a relationship?
  - Can you?
  - How will you go about it?

Looking for a challenge?

Try writing about one of our prompts with your friend(s)! See if you can come up with something together.

#95 – The world has been taken over by robots. (D) (H) (SF)

> ***Brainstorm …***
>
> - Is it just happening now, or has it been going on for a while?
>   - How long has it been?
>   - What is/was the transition like?
> - What is the society like?
> - Are they violent?
> - Are they benevolent?
> - Are humans trying to regain control?

Writing Exercise #19

Write about the first time you got a cellphone.

100

#96 – The latest phone has the craziest new feature. (SL) (R) (D)

Brainstorm ...

- What kind of feature?
  - What does it do?
  - Is it helpful or harmful?
- Is it already added, or do you have to pay for it?
- What does the phone look like?
- How many people have it?
  - What are they saying about it?
    - Are they allowed to talk about it?

Did you know?

We also make books to help with storytelling. With help on things like creating characters, world-building, magic systems, and more!

You can find more information on our website, www.TCStudiosHQ.com.

#97 – You've ripped out your tracker chip. Now what? (AA) (SF) (D)

Brainstorm ...

- Where was it?
- Who put it there?
    - Do you know?
- How did you get it out?
- Why was it put there?
- Why did you take it out?
- Does anyone know you took it out?
- What are you going to do now?

Did you know?

We also publish novels and comics that you can read!

You can find more information on our website,
www.TCStudiosHQ.com.

#98 – An injector is pumping poison into the Earth. (SF) (M) (F)

Brainstorm …

- Where did the injector come from?
  - Who or what put it there?
- How fast is the poison spreading?
- What is happening to the area around the injector?
- Is anyone trying to stop it?
  - How
  - What would the process be like?
  - Is anyone or anything defending it?
    - Will there be a fight?

Do you want to give us a prompt for next year's edition?

You can submit prompt ideas you have based on next year's chapter themes. Credit will be given if selected.

You can find more information on our website,
www.TCStudiosHQ.com.

#99 – You wake up in the hospital with a mechanical arm. (SF) (AA) (R)

Brainstorm ...

- Do you remember going to the hospital?
- Do you remember going under for surgery?
- What's moving your new arm like?
    - Can you move it?
- Does it look human? Or robotic?
- Does it have any extra features?
- Does it detach?

Did you know?

We post daily writing & drawing prompts on our Social Medias for everyone to participate in.

Find us @PromptParty and use #PromptParty.

You can find more information on our website, www.TCStudiosHQ.com.

#100 – Your brain has been downloaded into a robotic body. (SF) (R) (D)

Brainstorm ...

- Did you know about it, or did you wake up in that body?
- Why was it downloaded?
    - Was your human body dying?
    - Were you part of an experiment?
- What's it like being in the body?
    - Can you move it yet?
    - Can you feel anything?
    - What does the body look like?
    - What features does it have?

Writing Exercise #20

Write about a piece of technology you want to learn how to use.

#101 – Someone is wiping all the evidence from your hard drives. (M) (AA) (SF)

> **Brainstorm ...**
>
> - What evidence was/is on the hard drives?
> - What would it prove?
> - Who is erasing the data?
>   - Why?
>   - How?
> - How fast is it being erased?
> - Is there anything you can do to stop it?
>   - What?
>   - How?

Did you know?

In addition to posting daily on Social Media, we have daily interactive posts on our YouTube channel, Podcast, and Blog.

You can find more information on our website, www.TCStudiosHQ.com.

#102 – Your record player is repeating very specific phrases. (M) (SF) (H)

Brainstorm …

- What phrases?
- Are they in a certain order?
- Are they being played backwards?
- Does it start and stop at certain times?
- What does it mean?
    - Does it mean anything?
    - Is it just broken?
- Is someone controlling it?

Remember!

The listed genres/mediums and brainstorming boxes are **only suggestions!** We encourage you to do/use whatever you want.

#103 – You're in a toy store when all of the remote-control cars start heading towards you. (F) (AA) (H)

Brainstorm …

- How big are the toys?
- How fast are they going?
- Will you run away?
- Will you kick them away?
- Why are they coming towards you?
- Who's controlling them?

Be The First To Know.

Join our newsletter and be the first to know about new prompt books, novels, comics, giveaways, freebies, coupons, and anything else we've got going on!

Find our newsletter on our website, www.TCStudiosHQ.com.

\#104 – All technology has been outlawed. (D) (SF) (R)

Brainstorm …

- Why?
- Is it putting people in danger?
- Is the government hoarding it for themselves?
- How are people living now?
- How has it changed society?
    - Everyday living?

You can share your work with us on Facebook, Instagram & Twitter!

Tag us @PromptParty and use #PromptParty.

We'd love to see what you come up with!

#105 – All technology has been strictly reserved for the upper-class. (D) (AA) (SL)

Brainstorm ...

- How are the lower-class living without it?
  - Are any of them rebelling?
- What would they do to try to get the tech back?
- Are any of the lower-class stashing tech for themselves?
  - What kind?
  - How are they getting them?
    - Black market?
    - Theft?
  - What happens if they get caught?
- How do the upper-class feel about this?
  - Are any of them rebelling?
- How are their lives different?

Writing Exercise #21

Write about what you would do with a humanoid robot.

#106 – The government is hiding technology lightyears beyond what the masses have access to. (SF) (M) (D)

Brainstorm …

- What can this technology do?
- Where did they get it?
  - Did they create it?
  - Did they steal it from aliens?
  - Did they discover it here on Earth?
    - In ruins? Temples?
- What are they doing with it?
- What if someone finds out?

Do you want your work published?

You can submit any work made using our prompts to our annual anthologies! Published submissions receive shared 25% royalties.

You can find more information on our website, www.TCStudiosHQ.com.

#107 – Humans have created a serum for immortality. (SF) (R) (S)

Brainstorm …

- What did it take to create?
  - What ingredients?
  - Is there another cost?
  - Is there a consequence?
    - Are there several?
- Are they handing it out or keeping it for themselves?
  - How are they doing either?

Did you know?

A percentage of every anthology sold goes towards helping communities like yours. This includes donations to charities, funding of scholarships, creating of programs, and more!

You can find more information on our website, www.TCStudiosHQ.com.

#108 – You're on a team trying to stop an asteroid from colliding with Earth. (SF) (AA) (M)

> ### Brainstorm ...
>
> - How long until collision?
> - How big is the team trying to stop it?
>   - Who does it include?
> - How are you going about figuring out a solution?
>   - What are some of the ideas?
>   - Are any of the viable?
>   - Is there an evacuation plan?

Did you know?

In addition to our annual prompt anthologies, every year we have themed anthologies that you can also submit to!

You can find more information on our website, www.TCStudiosHQ.com.

#109 – While showering, you find an "on/off" tattoo on your body. (SF) (AA) (M)

Brainstorm ...

- Where is it located?
- Why are you just now finding it?
- Will you press it?
    - What happens when you do?
- Was it a drunken tattoo?

Looking for a challenge?

Try writing about one of our prompts with your friend(s)! See if you can come up with something together.

#110 – You're working on something that could win your side the war. (AA) (SF) (F)

Brainstorm ...

- What is it?
  - What does it do?
  - How would it help?
  - How long before it's done?
- What is the war about?
- How long has it been going on for?
- How desperate is your side to win?
- Is your side good or bad?
  - Is there a good side?
  - Is there a bad side?

Writing Exercise #22

Write about what you would do if you found a piece of alien technology.

#111 – Your computer screen goes black. A message appears. (M) (R) (D)

Brainstorm …

- What is the message?
- How fast is it appearing?
- What language is it in?
- Are there any images with it?
- What will you do with the message?
- Did anyone else see it?
- Who sent it?
    - Why to you?
    - Do you know them?
    - Is the message signed?

Did you know?

We also make books to help with storytelling. With help on things like creating characters, world-building, magic systems, and more!

You can find more information on our website, www.TCStudiosHQ.com.

#112 – You volunteer to test the newest technological breakthrough – but something goes wrong. (SL) (SF) (H)

Brainstorm ...

- What is the breakthrough?
    - What is it supposed to do?
- What went wrong?
- Did it go wrong with anyone else?
- What's happening?
- Is anyone doing anything about it?
    - Why or why not?

Did you know?

We also publish novels and comics that you can read!

You can find more information on our website, www.TCStudiosHQ.com.

#113 – A robot comes to your home and shows you a projection of someone asking for help. (SF) (AA) (M)

Brainstorm …

- What does the robot look like?
    - Is it short or tall?
    - What color is it?
- Does it speak?
- Who is in the projection?
    - Do you know them?
    - What are they saying?
- What will you do now?

Do you want to give us a prompt for next year's edition?

You can submit prompt ideas you have based on next year's chapter themes. Credit will be given if selected.

You can find more information on our website,
www.TCStudiosHQ.com.

#114 – You find a foreign piece of technology. It almost seems … alien. (SF) (M) (F)

Brainstorm …

- Where did you find it?
- Is there anyone else around it?
- Is/was it protected?
- Is it on or off?
  - Does it turn on?
- What does it look like?
- Is it big?
- Is it heavy?
- Is there anything written on it?
- What are you going to do with it?

Did you know?

We post daily writing & drawing prompts on our Social Medias for everyone to participate in.

Find us @PromptParty and use #PromptParty.

You can find more information on our website, www.TCStudiosHQ.com.

#115 – "Technology is great when it decides to work." (R) (P) (S)

Brainstorm …

- What isn't working?
- Does something stop working often?
    - Why?
    - What's causing it to stop working?
    - Is someone sabotaging it?
    - Is it too old?
    - Is it just a bad piece of tech?

Writing Exercise #23

What would you invent if you were an inventor?

120

#116 – You toss something in a pile at the junk yard and something turns on. (SF) (D) (M)

Brainstorm …

- What are you doing in a junk yard?
- What did you throw?
- What turned on?
- Where is it?
- Are you going to pick it up?
- What does it do?
- What happens after it turns on?

Did you know?

In addition to posting daily on Social Media, we have daily interactive posts on our YouTube channel, Podcast, and Blog.

You can find more information on our website, www.TCStudiosHQ.com.

#117 – "Dammit! Why won't this stupid thing work?!" (AA) (S) (P)

Brainstorm ...

- What isn't working?
- Why isn't it working?
- What do you need it to do?
- What happens if you can't get it to work?
  - What if you can?

Remember!

The listed genres/mediums and brainstorming boxes are **only suggestions!** We encourage you to do/use whatever you want.

#118 – Planned obsoletion. (SL) (D) (M)

Brainstorm ...

- Of what?
  - o Phones?
  - o Computers?
  - o People?
- Is there any way to counteract it?
- Who is behind it?

Be The First To Know.

Join our newsletter and be the first to know about new prompt books, novels, comics, giveaways, freebies, coupons, and anything else we've got going on!

Find our newsletter on our website, www.TCStudiosHQ.com.

#119 – "We didn't have this back in my day." (SF) (F) (S)

Brainstorm ...

- Have what?
  - o What are they talking about?
- Who are they talking to?
- How old are they?
  - o How old is the person/people they're talking to?
- Are they happy about the thing they didn't have?
  - o Do they curse it?

You can share your work with us on Facebook, Instagram & Twitter!

Tag us @PromptParty and use #PromptParty.

We'd love to see what you come up with!

#120 – This new tech is going to change the world. (SL) (M) (D)

Brainstorm ...

- What is the new tech?
  - What does it do?
- How is it going to change the world??
  - Will it be for the worse or for the better?
- Who is creating the tech?
- Do people know what's about to happen?

Writing Exercise #24

What would happen if all technology suddenly stopped working?

#121 – People's memories are being erased. (SF) (H) (M)

Brainstorm …

- How?
- Why?
    - Is there a purpose?
    - Is it a disease?
- Is it specific people or anyone?
- Is someone behind it?
    - Is anyone trying to stop them?
    - How?
    - Can they?

Do you want your work published?

You can submit any work made using our prompts to our annual anthologies! Published submissions receive shared 25% royalties.

You can find more information on our website, www.TCStudiosHQ.com.

Chapter Five: Places.

#122 – Area 51 is nothing like you expected. (R) (SF) (S)

Brainstorm ...

- What did you expect?
- What did you find instead?
- Is it a positive change or a negative one?
- Why are you there?
  - Is it by accident?
    - How did you get there?

Did you know?

A percentage of every anthology sold goes towards helping communities like yours. This includes donations to charities, funding of scholarships, creating of programs, and more!

You can find more information on our website, www.TCStudiosHQ.com.

#123 – You've just broken out of your containment module. (M) (AA) (D)

Brainstorm …

- Why were you in a containment module?
  - Was it for your safety?
  - Was it for the safety of others?
- Why did you break out?
- How did you?
  - Did someone or something help you?
- What are you going to do now?

Did you know?

In addition to our annual prompt anthologies, every year we have themed anthologies that you can also submit to!

You can find more information on our website, www.TCStudiosHQ.com.

#124 – "How the hell did I end up here?" (M) (SL) (AA)

Brainstorm …

- End up where?
  - ○ Where exactly are you?
  - ○ Do you know?
- Is anyone else there?
- Do you have any guesses as to how you got there?
  - ○ Any ideas why?
- Do you want to leave?
  - ○ How will you do that?
  - ○ Will anyone try to stop you?
- Do you want to stay?
  - ○ What will you do if you do?

Looking for a challenge?

Try writing about one of our prompts with your friend(s)! See if you can come up with something together.

#125 – You've just won a vacation to your favorite place. (R) (SL) (H)

Brainstorm ...

- What place?
  - o   Why is it your favorite?
- How did you win?
  - o   Did you enter a contest?
  - o   Win the lottery?
- How long is the vacation?
- Can you bring anyone else?
- What are you going to do there?

Writing Exercise #25

What if a new continent was discovered?

130

#126 – "… Where are we?" (H) (M) (F)

Brainstorm …

- Who's we?
    - Who is with you?
    - Are you referring to yourself?
- How are you going to go about figuring out where you are?
- Is there a way out?
- Are you out in the open?
- How is it that you don't know where you are?
    - Did something happen to prevent you from knowing?

Did you know?

We also make books to help with storytelling. With help on things like creating characters, world-building, magic systems, and more!

You can find more information on our website,
www.TCStudiosHQ.com.

#127 – You're on an alien planet – with no way to get back home. (S) (F) (SF)

Brainstorm …

- How did you get there?
- Why can't you leave?
- Is there any life on this planet?
  - If so, what is it like?
    - Does it come in various forms/species?
  - If not, how are you going to survive?
- Is anyone else with you?
- Does anyone on your home planet know you're here?

Did you know?

We also publish novels and comics that you can read!

You can find more information on our website,
www.TCStudiosHQ.com.

#128 – "How can they be in two places at once?" (M) (S) (AA)

Brainstorm ...

- Who or what is being questioned?
- What two places are they in?
    - What are they doing in either place?
        - Is it good, bad, or neutral?
- How might they be in two places at once?

Do you want to give us a prompt for next year's edition?

You can submit prompt ideas you have based on next year's chapter themes. Credit will be given if selected.

You can find more information on our website, www.TCStudiosHQ.com.

#129 – Next stop – the White House. (SL) (M) (D)

Brainstorm …

- What was the previous stop?
- Why is the White House the next stop?
  - What's the plan once they get there?
  - What's the purpose in going?
- Will it be easy to get there?
  - Will they be met with any challenges/obstacles?

Did you know?

We post daily writing & drawing prompts on our Social Medias for everyone to participate in.

Find us @PromptParty and use #PromptParty.

You can find more information on our website, www.TCStudiosHQ.com.

#130 – You need to find your way out of a locked room – and fast. (H) (P) (AA)

> **Brainstorm ...**
>
> - How did you get in the room?
> - Why is it locked?
> - Why do you need to get out in a hurry?
>   - What happens if you can't?
>   - What happens after you do?
> - Will anyone know if you escape?

Writing Exercise #26

Write about your spaceship traveling through a black hole.

#131 – A blind date is meeting you at a café in 20 minutes. (R) (M) (SL)

Brainstorm …

- Who set up the date?
    - A friend?
    - A family member?
    - A dating website/app?
- How do you feel about it?
    - Excited?
    - Nervous?
    - Dreadful?
- How are you dressed?

Remember!

The listed genres/mediums and brainstorming boxes are **only suggestions!** We encourage you to do/use whatever you want.

#132 – You're stranded on a deserted island. (AA) (H) (M)

Brainstorm …

- How did you get there?
- Do you have anything with you?
- Is anyone else with you?
- What are your first steps to survival?
- Have you been there for long?
  - If so, how long?
- Is there anything dangerous on the island?
- Are you working towards getting off it?

You can share your work with us on Facebook, Instagram & Twitter!

Tag us @PromptParty and use #PromptParty.

We'd love to see what you come up with!

#133 – Road trip! (SL) (F) (R)

Brainstorm …

- Where are you going?
- Where did you leave from?
- What are you hoping to see along the way?
- Is anyone coming with you?
- Where are you going to sleep?
- What are you driving?

Do you want your work published?

You can submit any work made using our prompts to our annual anthologies! Published submissions receive shared 25% royalties.

You can find more information on our website, www.TCStudiosHQ.com.

#134 – This place feels totally different at night. (H) (P) (S)

Brainstorm ...

- What place?
  - Where are they/you?
- Is it a good or bad difference?
  - What does it mean for them if it's either?
- What was it like during the day?
- Was the change gradual or did it happen suddenly?

Did you know?

A percentage of every anthology sold goes towards helping communities like yours. This includes donations to charities, funding of scholarships, creating of programs, and more!

You can find more information on our website, www.TCStudiosHQ.com.

#135 – "Where did you last see them?" (M) (SL) (H)

Brainstorm ...

- Is someone missing?
- Did someone run away?
- Were they kidnapped?
- Who is asking?
    - The police?
        - A detective?
    - A parent?
    - A chaperone?
- Is there limited time to find them?
    - What happens if that time runs out?

Writing Exercise #27

Write about finding a lost child.

140

#136 – Go to your happy place. They won't find you there. (F) (S) (D)

Brainstorm ...

- Where is your happy place?
- Is it a physical place or metaphorical?
- How do you get there?
- Who don't you want to find you?
- What happens if they do find you?
- Who else is in this place?

Did you know?

In addition to our annual prompt anthologies, every year we have <u>themed</u> anthologies that you can also submit to!

You can find more information on our website, www.TCStudiosHQ.com.

#137 – Were you just … teleported? (SF) (F) (AA)

> ### *Brainstorm …*
>
> - Where were you teleported to?
> - Where were you teleported from?
> - Who or what teleported you?
> - How do you feel after being teleported?
>   - Nauseous? Jumpy?
>   - Are any body parts missing?
> - Do you want to go back to where you came from?
>   - How are you going to do that?
> - Do you want to stay where you ended up?
>   - Why?

Looking for a challenge?

Try doing one of our prompts with your friend(s)! See if you can come up with something together.

#138 – You're at the wrong place at the wrong time. (H) (S) (D)

Brainstorm …

- Where is that?
- Why is it at the wrong time?
- What's happening?
- Can you leave?
    - Would someone or something try to stop you?
- What happens if you stay?

Did you know?

We also make books to help with storytelling. With help on things like creating characters, world-building, magic systems, and more!

You can find more information on our website, www.TCStudiosHQ.com.

#139 – "Where you go, I go." (AA) (P) (R)

Brainstorm …

- Where who goes?
    - Why are you so willing to follow them?
    - Where might they be going?
    - Did they want you to stay behind?

Did you know?

We also publish novels and comics that you can read!

You can find more information on our website,
www.TCStudiosHQ.com.

#140 – Someone offers to take you to a magical place. Will you go? (F) (AA) (S)

Brainstorm ...

- Who is offering?
- How are they going to get you there?
- What makes it so magical?
- Will you go?
    - Why or why not?
    - What could happen if you do?
    - What could happen if you don't?

Writing Exercise #28

Write about being teleported.

145

#141 – "Where are you taking me?" (M) (H) (SL)

Brainstorm …

- Who is taking you?
- How?
  - By foot?
  - By car?
  - By horseback?
- Did you go willingly?
- Are you being kidnapped?
- How is this being said?
  - With fear?
  - Romantically?
  - With annoyance?

Do you want to give us a prompt for next year's edition?

You can submit prompt ideas you have based on next year's chapter themes. Credit will be given if selected.

You can find more information on our website, www.TCStudiosHQ.com.

#142 – "Where the hell do you think you're going?" (SL) (SF) (AA)

Brainstorm ...

- Who is trying to leave?
- Why?
  - Is it in jest?
  - Are they trying to run for their life?
  - Are they walking away from an argument?
- Is this person going to try to stop them from leaving?
  - How?

Did you know?

We post daily writing & drawing prompts on our Social Medias for everyone to participate in.

Find us @PromptParty and use #PromptParty.

You can find more information on our website, www.TCStudiosHQ.com.

#143 – You've just woken up in the hospital with no memory of how you got there. (M) (P) (R)

Brainstorm ...

- Where is the hospital?
    - o   Is it in an area you know?
    - o   Are you in a different town/city?
- Is the person/people that brought you there in the room when you wake up?
- Will they tell you the truth or lie about the situation?
- Try writing a flashback leading up to this point or writing a short series of scene that lead the character to regain their memory.

Did you know?

In addition to posting daily on Social Media, we have daily interactive posts on our YouTube channel, Podcast, and Blog.

You can find more information on our website, www.TCStudiosHQ.com.

#144 – "This isn't the time or the place for that." (SL) (F) (D)

> **Brainstorm ...**
>
> - What is being done?
>   - Why shouldn't it be?
>   - What should be done instead?

Remember!

The listed genres/mediums and brainstorming boxes are **only suggestions!** We encourage you to do/use whatever you want.

#145 – "Meet me in the lobby in 10 minutes." (M) (AA) (S)

Brainstorm ...

- Meet who?
    - Is it someone you know?
    - If not, who is it?
- Why do they want to meet in the lobby?
- Do you want to meet them?
    - Do you have a choice?
    - What happens if you do?
    - What happens if you don't?

Writing Exercise #29

Write about heading off on an adventure at sea.

#146 – You are undeniably, undoubtably, indescribably – lost. (M) (SL) (R)

Brainstorm ...

- Where were you coming from?
- Where are you trying to get to?
- How did you get so lost?
- Were you following a map or GPS?
- Is there anyone else with you?
- Are you worried?
- Is there anyone around that can help you?

Be The First To Know.

Join our newsletter and be the first to know about new prompt books, novels, comics, giveaways, freebies, coupons, and anything else we've got going on!

Find our newsletter on our website, www.TCStudiosHQ.com.

#147 – So this is what heaven looks like. (S) (F) (SL)

Brainstorm ...

- Is this statement literal or figurative?
- Either way, what does heaven look like?
- How did this person get there?

You can share your work with us on Facebook, Instagram & Twitter!

Tag us @PromptParty and use #PromptParty.

We'd love to see what you come up with!

#148 – So this is what hell looks like. (SL) (S) (F)

Brainstorm ...

- Is this statement literal or figurative?
- Either way, what does hell look like?
- How did this person get there?

Do you want your work published?

You can submit any work made using our prompts to our annual anthologies! Published submissions receive shared 25% royalties.

You can find more information on our website, www.TCStudiosHQ.com.

#149 – "I just want to go home." (H) (AA) (D)

Brainstorm …

- Where are they?
- Who are they?
  - A child, teen, or adult?
- Why do they want to go home?
- How long has it been since they've been home?
- Are they having a bad time where they are?
- Is there someone or something they miss at home?

Did you know?

A percentage of every anthology sold goes towards helping communities like yours. This includes donations to charities, funding of scholarships, creating of programs, and more!

You can find more information on our website,
www.TCStudiosHQ.com.

#150 – You've got the map – now you just need someone who can read it. (AA) (F) (D)

Brainstorm ...

- Why can't you read it?
    - Is it too confusing?
    - Is it not in English?
- Do you know anyone that can read it?
    - Would they be willing to?
    - Would you have to pay them?
- How did you get this map in the first place?
    - Why do you want/need it?

Writing Exercise #30

Write about coming home from a long trip.

155

#151 – You never thought you'd be on the other side of a prison cell. (SL) (AA) (S)

Brainstorm …

- Which side?
    - Inside or out?
- If in, what have you done to get yourself put inside a prison cell?
- If out, what in your life has changed that you are now walking free?
- What are you going to do now that you're on either side?

Did you know?

In addition to our annual prompt anthologies, every year we have themed anthologies that you can also submit to!

You can find more information on our website, www.TCStudiosHQ.com.

#152 – "Ugh, I don't want to go." (SL) (P) (M)

Brainstorm …

- Go where?
- Why don't you want to go?
  - Are you being forced to?
  - Will there be consequences if you don't go?
  - Is there somewhere you want to be instead?

Looking for a challenge?

Try doing one of our prompts with your friend(s)! See if you can come up with something together.

Chapter Six: Science.

#153 – You've discovered the cure for cancer – inside a government vault. (SF) (M) (D)

Brainstorm …

- Do you work for the government?
  - How did you find the vault?
  - How did you get in?
  - Are you a spy?
    - Part of some sort of rebellion?
- Did you know there would be a cure inside this vault?
  - Were you looking for something else at the time?
- What are you going to do now?
  - Will you try to share it with the masses?
    - Is there a finite amount?
    - How will you get the information out?
      - Will people try to stop you?

Did you know?

We also make books to help with storytelling. With help on things like creating characters, world-building, magic systems, and more!

You can find more information on our website, www.TCStudiosHQ.com.

#154 – Something's growing in your boss' lab. (H) (SF) (S)

Brainstorm ...

- What is it?
  - o Is it human? An animal? Something else entirely?
- Is it out in the open, or did you find it hidden away?
- Is it safe?
- Is it legal?
- What are you going to do now that you've seen it?
  - o Turn them in?
  - o Destroy it?
  - o Join the project?

Did you know?

We also publish novels and comics that you can read!

You can find more information on our website,
www.TCStudiosHQ.com.

#155 – Scientists have figured out how to bring the dead back to life. (P) (SF) (H)

Brainstorm ...

- How?
    - What is needed to do it?
- What are the dead like when they come back?
    - Can they speak?
    - Do they need new organs?
        - Do they work?
    - Do they remember dying?
    - Do they have any weird of concerning new traits?
- Why are they doing this?

Writing Exercise #31

Write about volunteering for an experiment.

#156 – A new metal has been discovered – and it's being used in … interesting ways. (SF) (M) (D)

Brainstorm …

- Where was this metal discovered?
- What traits and properties does it have?
- How is it being used?
    - Is its use concerning?
    - Is it to be celebrated?
- How much of this metal is there to be harvested?
    - Is it plentiful?
    - Is it finite?

Do you want to give us a prompt for next year's edition?

You can submit prompt ideas you have based on next year's chapter themes. Credit will be given if selected.

You can find more information on our website, www.TCStudiosHQ.com.

#157 – There is now a weekly pill you can take to keep you from aging. (D) (SF) (SL)

Brainstorm …

- How was this created?
- Who invested it?
  - Why?
- What ingredients might be in it?
- Are there any side effects?
- How much does this pill cost?
- How old do you have to be to start?

Did you know?

We post daily writing & drawing prompts on our Social Medias for everyone to participate in.

Find us @PromptParty and use #PromptParty.

You can find more information on our website, www.TCStudiosHQ.com.

#158 – The internet is now at your fingertips – literally. (R) (AA) (S)

Brainstorm …

- What does this mean?
  - What are the applications?
- What is the process to have the internet at your fingertips?
- Are there any negative effects?
- What are the positive results?
- How does this effect daily living? Society?
- Are there any restrictions? Bugs?

Did you know?

In addition to posting daily on Social Media, we have daily interactive posts on our YouTube channel, Podcast, and Blog.

You can find more information on our website,
www.TCStudiosHQ.com.

#159 – Some kids in your neighbor's garage may or may not have just successfully created a teleportation machine. (SF) (SL) (F)

Brainstorm ...

- Who are the kids?
- Do their parents know?
- Are they human?
- How did you find out about it?
- What are you going to do now that you've seen it?
  - Are you going to report it?
  - Are you going to test it out?

Remember!

The listed genres/mediums and brainstorming boxes are **only suggestions!** We encourage you to do/use whatever you want.

#160 – "This breakthrough could save mankind." (D) (H) (M)

Brainstorm ...

- Is mankind in danger?
    - Why?
- What kind of breakthrough is it?
    - Medical?
    - Transportation?
- Who is behind the breakthrough?
- Is it completed or dies it still have some time to go before it's ready?

Writing Exercise #32

Write about doing research to find a cure.

#161 – The new scientist in your department is a little sketchy ... (M) (H) (SF)

Brainstorm ...

- Sketchy how?
    - Personality?
    - Intentions?
    - Practices?

Be The First To Know.

Join our newsletter and be the first to know about new prompt books, novels, comics, giveaways, freebies, coupons, and anything else we've got going on!

Find our newsletter on our website, www.TCStudiosHQ.com.

#162 – The world's greatest scientists have banded together to take over the world. (F) (AA) (SF)

Brainstorm ...

- Why?
- How?
- How did this all get started?
- What are they planning on doing with the world if they take it over?
  - ○ Something positive or negative?
- Is anyone trying to stop them?
  - ○ Can they be stopped?
- How many of them are there?

You can share your work with us on Facebook, Instagram & Twitter!

Tag us @PromptParty and use #PromptParty.

We'd love to see what you come up with!

#163 – Your scientific experiment is about to go horribly, horribly wrong. (F) (S) (P)

Brainstorm ...

- Why?
- Did you do something wrong?
- Did you do something right?
- Did someone else?
- Was it outside of your control?
    - Power going off?
    - A fire starting?
- Is there any way you can stop it?
    - How?
    - Do you need help?

Do you want your work published?

You can submit any work made using our prompts to our annual anthologies! Published submissions receive shared 25% royalties.

You can find more information on our website,
www.TCStudiosHQ.com.

#164 – Scientific law as we know it is falling apart. (D) (SF) (M)

> ## *Brainstorm ...*
>
> - What does that mean?
> - What's causing it?
> - What's happening because of it?
> - Is there any way to stop it?
>   - What if there isn't?

Did you know?

A percentage of every anthology sold goes towards helping communities like yours. This includes donations to charities, funding of scholarships, creating of programs, and more!

You can find more information on our website, www.TCStudiosHQ.com.

#165 – Aliens have agreed to share their scientific knowledge with us. (SF) (F) (S)

Brainstorm …

- What kind of knowledge?
- Is this a mistake?
  - Are we ready and able to handle such information?
- How will it change our lives?
  - Will it be negative or positive?
- What are the aliens' intentions?
- Under what circumstances are they agreeing to share this knowledge?
  - Are they being threatened?
  - Are they being generous?
  - Are they being mischievous?

Writing Exercise #33

Write about the process to bring someone or something back to life.

170

#166 – "Good god ... what have you done?!" (R) (H) (M)

Brainstorm ...

- What's been done?
- Are there going to be consequences because of it?
  - What kind?
  - Is there any way to reverse it?

Did you know?

In addition to our annual prompt anthologies, every year we have
<u>themed</u> anthologies that you can also submit to!

You can find more information on our website,
www.TCStudiosHQ.com.

#167 – Science has been set back by 50 years. (M) (D) (SF)

Brainstorm ...

- What does this mean for us?
    - For our society?
    - For our means of communication and travel?
    - For our medical practices?
- What's being done to recover our lost progress?

Looking for a challenge?

Try writing about one of our prompts with your friend(s)! See if you
can come up with something together.

#168 – The sun is going to explode millions of years ahead of schedule. (H) (SF) (M)

Brainstorm ...

- Is there a predicted date that this will happen?
- Will we abandon Earth?
- Do we have any chance for survival?

Did you know?

We also make books to help with storytelling. With help on things like creating characters, world-building, magic systems, and more!

You can find more information on our website, www.TCStudiosHQ.com.

#169 – Scientists have figured out how to bring extinct animals back to life by using their remains to create clones. (SF) (SL) (AA)

Brainstorm …

- Which animals are they bringing back?
- What does this mean for our ecosystem?
- Is it a mistake to have brought some of them back?
  - Which ones?

Did you know?

We also publish novels and comics that you can read!

You can find more information on our website,
www.TCStudiosHQ.com.

#170 – "If only we had the money to fund our research …" (SL) (R) (D)

Brainstorm …

- What kind of research do they need to be funded?
  - Are there any lives at stake?
- Where might they get the money they need?
- What are they willing to do to get it?

Writing Exercise #34

Write about finding ancient technology.

#171 – The moon is starting to leave Earth's orbit. (SF) (H) (M)

Brainstorm ...

- Why is this happening?
- How is it happening?
- Can anything be done about it?
- What's going to happen to Earth if it loses its moon?

Do you want to give us a prompt for next year's edition?

You can submit prompt ideas you have based on next year's chapter themes. Credit will be given if selected.

You can find more information on our website, www.TCStudiosHQ.com.

#172 – "There appears to be a chemical reaction happening …" (P) (S) (R)

Brainstorm …

- Happening to what?
- What kind of chemical reaction?
- Is it dangerous?
- Should people be removed from the area?

Did you know?

We post daily writing & drawing prompts on our Social Medias for everyone to participate in.

Find us @PromptParty and use #PromptParty.

You can find more information on our website, www.TCStudiosHQ.com.

#173 – What would Earth be like one thousand years into the future? (D) (M) (SF)

Brainstorm ...

- What kind of technology might we have?
- What kind of medical advancements might have been made?
- How might society have changed?
  - For the better or worse?
- How might the environment and ozone have changed?
  - For the better or worse?

Did you know?

In addition to posting daily on Social Media, we have daily interactive posts on our YouTube channel, Podcast, and Blog.

You can find more information on our website, www.TCStudiosHQ.com.

#174 – What would your field of research be if you were a scientist? (SL) (R) (F)

Brainstorm …

- What would you choose and why?
  - Do you think you'd enjoy the work?
  - Do you think it would be difficult?
- What work would you hope to do?
  - What changes or discoveries would you hope to make?

Remember!

The listed genres/mediums and brainstorming boxes are **only suggestions!** We encourage you to do/use whatever you want.

#175 – Climate change has set the world in crisis. (H) (D) (SL)

Brainstorm …

- What's happening because of it?
- What or who is to blame?
- What is being done to combat the crisis?
- Is the planet too far gone to save?
    - Are humans going to abandon it?

Writing Exercise #35

Write about a device that is threatening humanity.

180

#176 – "We've done it! We've found the cure!" (SF) (S) (M)

Brainstorm ...

- Who's done it?
- What have they found the cure to?
- Who needs it?
- How are they going to get it to them?
- Are they going to charge for it?
- How long have they been working on this cure?

Be The First To Know.

Join our newsletter and be the first to know about new prompt books, novels, comics, giveaways, freebies, coupons, and anything else we've got going on!

Find our newsletter on our website, www.TCStudiosHQ.com.

#177 – A device that allows people to control others as if they were a videogame character. (R) (SL) (SF)

Brainstorm ...

- Where is the device located on the body?
- How long does the device last?
- Is there a way to opt out once it starts?
- What if it malfunctions?
- Has this been used to commit any crimes?

You can share your work with us on Facebook, Instagram & Twitter!

Tag us @PromptParty and use #PromptParty.

We'd love to see what you come up with!

#178 – A device that lets you slow or quicken your eyes frame rate. (F) (AA) (D)

Brainstorm ...

- Where is the device located?
- How long does it last?
- Is there a way to stop it once it starts?
- What if it malfunctions?

Do you want your work published?

You can submit any work made using our prompts to our annual anthologies! Published submissions receive shared 25% royalties.

You can find more information on our website,
www.TCStudiosHQ.com.

#179 – Never fall in love with your experiments. (R) (H) (M)

> ***Brainstorm …***
>
> - Why not?
>   - What could go wrong?
>   - Is it illegal?
>   - What if you did anyway?
>   - What would you have to do?
>   - Would you keep it a secret?

Did you know?

A percentage of every anthology sold goes towards helping communities like yours. This includes donations to charities, funding of scholarships, creating of programs, and more!

You can find more information on our website, www.TCStudiosHQ.com.

#180 – "This defies everything we know of space and time." (S) (AA) (SF)

> **Brainstorm ...**
>
> - What have they just found out?
> - Who is there to discover it?
> - What does this mean for what we know of space and time?
>   - How has it changed with this new information?
>   - Is the information accurate?

Writing Exercise #36

Write about scientists trying to understand magic.

#181 – A scientist has just discovered the secret to immortality but is hesitant to reveal it to the world. (M) (H) (SF)

Brainstorm …

- What is the secret?
  - How did they discover it?
- Why are they so hesitant?
- What could revealing it to the public do?
- What could revealing it to their colleagues do?

Did you know?

In addition to our annual prompt anthologies, every year we have themed anthologies that you can also submit to!

You can find more information on our website, www.TCStudiosHQ.com.

#182 – Your spaceship has blown an engine on your way to your destination. (SF) (AA) (SL)

Brainstorm …

- Can your ship still function with one less engine?
    - Is it in danger of exploding?
    - Is it in danger of crashing?
- Are there any repairs that can be done while you're still in motion?
- Who is on board?
- Where are you headed?
- Where did you come from?

Looking for a challenge?

Try writing about one of our prompts with your friend(s)! See if you can come up with something together.

#183 – "Tell Dr. Garner I'll be with him in a moment." (SL) (S) (P)

Brainstorm …

- Who is speaking?
- What are they doing that they can't see Dr. Garner right now?
- Who is Dr. Garner?
    o Why are they there to see them?

Did you know?

We also make books to help with storytelling. With help on things like creating characters, world-building, magic systems, and more!

You can find more information on our website, www.TCStudiosHQ.com.

Chapter Seven: Emotion.

#184 – Rage. (AA) (F) (R)

Brainstorm ...

- What's causing this emotion?
- How is it being expressed?
    - ○ Is it healthy or unhealthy?
- How can it be changed?
- Is anyone else involved?

Did you know?

We also publish novels and comics that you can read!

You can find more information on our website,
www.TCStudiosHQ.com.

#185 – Uncertainty. (M) (P) (D)

> ### Brainstorm ...
>
> - What's causing this emotion?
> - How is it being expressed?
>   - Is it healthy or unhealthy?
> - How can it be changed?
> - Is anyone else involved?

Writing Exercise #37

Write about someone discovering love for the first time.

#186 – Love. (R) (SL) (F)

Brainstorm ...

- What's causing this emotion?
- How is it being expressed?
  - Is it healthy or unhealthy?
- How can it be changed?
- Is anyone else involved?

Do you want to give us a prompt for next year's edition?

You can submit prompt ideas you have based on next year's chapter themes. Credit will be given if selected.

You can find more information on our website, www.TCStudiosHQ.com.

#187 – Desperation. (H) (D) (P)

Brainstorm ...

- What's causing this emotion?
- How is it being expressed?
  - Is it healthy or unhealthy?
- How can it be changed?
- Is anyone else involved?

Did you know?

We post daily writing & drawing prompts on our Social Medias for everyone to participate in.

Find us @PromptParty and use #PromptParty.

You can find more information on our website, www.TCStudiosHQ.com.

#188 – Sorrow. (AA) (F) (M)

Brainstorm …

- What's causing this emotion?
- How is it being expressed?
    - Is it healthy or unhealthy?
- How can it be changed?
- Is anyone else involved?

Remember!

The listed genres/mediums and brainstorming boxes are **only suggestions!** We encourage you to do/use whatever you want.

#189 – Relief. (M) (SL) (S)

Brainstorm …

- What's causing this emotion?
- How is it being expressed?
    - Is it healthy or unhealthy?
- How can it be changed?
- Is anyone else involved?

You can share your work with us on Facebook, Instagram & Twitter!

Tag us @PromptParty and use #PromptParty.

We'd love to see what you come up with!

#190 – Regret. (AA) (SF) (H)

Brainstorm …

- What's causing this emotion?
- How is it being expressed?
    - Is it healthy or unhealthy?
- How can it be changed?
- Is anyone else involved?

Writing Exercise #38

Write about someone expressing rage.

#191 – Joy. (R) (S) (SL)

Brainstorm …

- What's causing this emotion?
- How is it being expressed?
  - Is it healthy or unhealthy?
- How can it be changed?
- Is anyone else involved?

Do you want your work published?

You can submit any work made using our prompts to our annual anthologies! Published submissions receive shared 25% royalties.

You can find more information on our website, www.TCStudiosHQ.com.

#192 – Denial. (M) (H) (D)

Brainstorm ...

- What's causing this emotion?
- How is it being expressed?
  - Is it healthy or unhealthy?
- How can it be changed?
- Is anyone else involved?

Did you know?

A percentage of every anthology sold goes towards helping communities like yours. This includes donations to charities, funding of scholarships, creating of programs, and more!

You can find more information on our website, www.TCStudiosHQ.com.

#193 – Curiosity. (SF) (F) (SL)

Brainstorm …

- What's causing this emotion?
- How is it being expressed?
  - Is it healthy or unhealthy?
- How can it be changed?
- Is anyone else involved?

Did you know?

In addition to our annual prompt anthologies, every year we have themed anthologies that you can also submit to!

You can find more information on our website, www.TCStudiosHQ.com.

#194 – Relaxed. (SL) (S) (R)

Brainstorm ...

- What's causing this emotion?
- How is it being expressed?
  - o Is it healthy or unhealthy?
- How can it be changed?
- Is anyone else involved?

Looking for a challenge?

Try doing one of our prompts with your friend(s)! See if you can come up with something together.

#195 – Stressed. (M) (H) (SL)

Brainstorm ...

- What's causing this emotion?
- How is it being expressed?
  - Is it healthy or unhealthy?
- How can it be changed?
- Is anyone else involved?

Writing Exercise #39

Write about someone showing loyalty.

#196 – Fatigue. (F) (D) (P)

Brainstorm ...

- What's causing this emotion?
- How is it being expressed?
    - Is it healthy or unhealthy?
- How can it be changed?
- Is anyone else involved?

Did you know?

We also make books to help with storytelling. With help on things like creating characters, world-building, magic systems, and more!

You can find more information on our website,
www.TCStudiosHQ.com.

#197 – Frustration. (R) (F) (M)

Brainstorm ...

- What's causing this emotion?
- How is it being expressed?
    - Is it healthy or unhealthy?
- How can it be changed?
- Is anyone else involved?

Did you know?

We also publish novels and comics that you can read!

You can find more information on our website,
www.TCStudiosHQ.com.

#198 – Hope. (F) (SL) (SF)

Brainstorm …

- What's causing this emotion?
- How is it being expressed?
  - ○ Is it healthy or unhealthy?
- How can it be changed?
- Is anyone else involved?

Do you want to give us a prompt for next year's edition?

You can submit prompt ideas you have based on next year's chapter themes. Credit will be given if selected.

You can find more information on our website,
www.TCStudiosHQ.com.

#199 – Lust. (S) (R) (F)

Brainstorm ...

- What's causing this emotion?
- How is it being expressed?
  - Is it healthy or unhealthy?
- How can it be changed?
- Is anyone else involved?

Did you know?

We post daily writing & drawing prompts on our Social Medias for everyone to participate in.

Find us @PromptParty and use #PromptParty.

You can find more information on our website, www.TCStudiosHQ.com.

#200 – Hatred. (SL) (P) (D)

Brainstorm ...

- What's causing this emotion?
- How is it being expressed?
  - Is it healthy or unhealthy?
- How can it be changed?
- Is anyone else involved?

Writing Exercise #40

Write about someone being scared.

#201 – Nostalgia. (S) (R) (AA)

Brainstorm ...

- What's causing this emotion?
- How is it being expressed?
  - Is it healthy or unhealthy?
- How can it be changed?
- Is anyone else involved?

Did you know?

In addition to posting daily on Social Media, we have daily interactive posts on our YouTube channel, Podcast, and Blog.

You can find more information on our website, www.TCStudiosHQ.com.

#202 – Guilt. (AA) (P) (SL)

Brainstorm …

- What's causing this emotion?
- How is it being expressed?
  - Is it healthy or unhealthy?
- How can it be changed?
- Is anyone else involved?

Remember!

The listed genres/mediums and brainstorming boxes are **only suggestions!** We encourage you to do/use whatever you want.

#203 – Depression. (SL) (D) (H)

Brainstorm …

- What's causing this emotion?
- How is it being expressed?
  - Is it healthy or unhealthy?
- How can it be changed?
- Is anyone else involved?

Be The First To Know.

Join our newsletter and be the first to know about new prompt books, novels, comics, giveaways, freebies, coupons, and anything else we've got going on!

Find our newsletter on our website, www.TCStudiosHQ.com.

#204 – Worry. (F) (M) (S)

Brainstorm ...

- What's causing this emotion?
- How is it being expressed?
  - Is it healthy or unhealthy?
- How can it be changed?
- Is anyone else involved?

You can share your work with us on Facebook, Instagram & Twitter!

Tag us @PromptParty and use #PromptParty.

We'd love to see what you come up with!

#205 – Cautious. (R) (AA) (P)

Brainstorm ...

- What's causing this emotion?
- How is it being expressed?
  - Is it healthy or unhealthy?
- How can it be changed?
- Is anyone else involved?

Writing Exercise #41

Write about someone working their way through three different emotions.

#206 – Selfish. (D) (SL) (SF)

> ### Brainstorm ...
>
> - What's causing this emotion?
> - How is it being expressed?
>   - Is it healthy or unhealthy?
> - How can it be changed?
> - Is anyone else involved?

Do you want your work published?

You can submit any work made using our prompts to our annual anthologies! Published submissions receive shared 25% royalties.

You can find more information on our website,
www.TCStudiosHQ.com.

#207 – Flirtatious. (R) (F) (SL)

Brainstorm …

- What's causing this emotion?
- How is it being expressed?
  - Is it healthy or unhealthy?
- How can it be changed?
- Is anyone else involved?

Did you know?

A percentage of every anthology sold goes towards helping communities like yours. This includes donations to charities, funding of scholarships, creating of programs, and more!

You can find more information on our website, www.TCStudiosHQ.com.

#208 – Giddy. (M) (H) (D)

Brainstorm ...

- What's causing this emotion?
- How is it being expressed?
    - Is it healthy or unhealthy?
- How can it be changed?
- Is anyone else involved?

Did you know?

In addition to our annual prompt anthologies, every year we have themed anthologies that you can also submit to!

You can find more information on our website, www.TCStudiosHQ.com.

#209 – Determined. (D) (AA) (S)

Brainstorm …

- What's causing this emotion?
- How is it being expressed?
    - Is it healthy or unhealthy?
- How can it be changed?
- Is anyone else involved?

Looking for a challenge?

Try doing one of our prompts with your friend(s)! See if you can come up with something together.

#210 – Defiant. (SF) (R) (SL)

Brainstorm …

- What's causing this emotion?
- How is it being expressed?
    - Is it healthy or unhealthy?
- How can it be changed?
- Is anyone else involved?

Writing Exercise #42

Write about someone causing an emotion in someone else.

#211 – Submissive. (M) (SL) (F)

Brainstorm …

- What's causing this emotion?
- How is it being expressed?
    - Is it healthy or unhealthy?
- How can it be changed?
- Is anyone else involved?

Did you know?

We also make books to help with storytelling. With help on things like creating characters, world-building, magic systems, and more!

You can find more information on our website, www.TCStudiosHQ.com.

#212 – Disappointed. (P) (AA) (SF)

Brainstorm ...

- What's causing this emotion?
- How is it being expressed?
    - Is it healthy or unhealthy?
- How can it be changed?
- Is anyone else involved?

Did you know?

We also publish novels and comics that you can read!

You can find more information on our website,
www.TCStudiosHQ.com.

#213 – Heartbroken. (R) (H) (M)

Brainstorm ...

- What's causing this emotion?
- How is it being expressed?
  - Is it healthy or unhealthy?
- How can it be changed?
- Is anyone else involved?

Do you want to give us a prompt for next year's edition?

You can submit prompt ideas you have based on next year's chapter themes. Credit will be given if selected.

You can find more information on our website, www.TCStudiosHQ.com.

#214 – Satisfied. (SL) (S) (R)

Brainstorm ...

- What's causing this emotion?
- How is it being expressed?
  - Is it healthy or unhealthy?
- How can it be changed?
- Is anyone else involved?

Did you know?

We post daily writing & drawing prompts on our Social Medias for everyone to participate in.

Find us @PromptParty and use #PromptParty.

You can find more information on our website, www.TCStudiosHQ.com.

Chapter Eight: Food.

#215 – Breakfast. (SL) (F) (R)

Brainstorm …

- What's being served?
  - Is it homemade?
    - Who's making it?
  - Is it fast food?
    - How much does it cost?
- Is it hot or cold?
- Is there a drink being served with it?

Writing Exercise #43

Write about opening your own restaurant.

#216 – You've got food poisoning. (M) (SF) (SL)

Brainstorm ...

- How?
    - What did you eat that caused it?
- Is it lasting a long time?
- What are the symptoms?
- What are you doing to treat it?
- Did you have to miss work?
- Is there anyone to take care of you?

Did you know?

In addition to posting daily on Social Media, we have daily interactive posts on our YouTube channel, Podcast, and Blog.

You can find more information on our website,
www.TCStudiosHQ.com.

#217 – "This is delicious!" (F) (S) (H)

Brainstorm …

- What is?
    - o What are they eating/drinking?
- Where are they eating it?
    - o At home?
    - o At someone else's home?
    - o At a restaurant?

Remember!

The listed genres/mediums and brainstorming boxes are **only suggestions!** We encourage you to do/use whatever you want.

#218 – You've just been accepted into the culinary school of your dreams. (SL) (AA) (D)

Brainstorm …

- Have you been studying/practicing hard to get in?
  - How have you been studying/practicing?
- How many other students are there?
- What kinds of things are you going to learn?
- Where is the school?
- How much does it cost?
- Can you do an internship while you're there?

Be The First To Know.

Join our newsletter and be the first to know about new prompt books, novels, comics, giveaways, freebies, coupons, and anything else we've got going on!

Find our newsletter on our website, www.TCStudiosHQ.com.

#219 – You have an apprenticeship with your favorite chef. (R) (S) (P)

Brainstorm ...

- What is this chef known for?
    - What kinds of things do they cook?
    - How many restaurants do they have?
- How did you get the apprenticeship?
    - How long is it?
    - What does it entail?
    - Is it paid?
    - Where is it?

You can share your work with us on Facebook, Instagram & Twitter!

Tag us @PromptParty and use #PromptParty.

We'd love to see what you come up with!

#220 – You start as a waiter tomorrow night. (M) (AA) (F)

Brainstorm ...

- Where are you working?
- Is it a good place?
- Do people tip well?
- What time is your shift?
- Is there a uniform?
- Do you know anyone that works there?
- Do you know any of the customers?

Writing Exercise #44

Write about being poisoned.

#221 – Dessert. (R) (SL) (D)

> **Brainstorm ...**
>
> - Cake?
> - Pie?
> - Ice cream?
> - What flavors?
> - What toppings?

Do you want your work published?

You can submit any work made using our prompts to our annual anthologies! Published submissions receive shared 25% royalties.

You can find more information on our website, www.TCStudiosHQ.com.

#222 – "I'm so sick of this packaged dehydrated crap." (SF) (D) (AA)

> ### *Brainstorm ...*
>
> - Why are they eating dehydrated meals?
> - Are they in space?
> - Are they surviving off them?
> - How long have they been eating it?
> - Do they know when they'll have something else?

Did you know?

A percentage of every anthology sold goes towards helping communities like yours. This includes donations to charities, funding of scholarships, creating of programs, and more!

You can find more information on our website, www.TCStudiosHQ.com.

#223 – Your partner has surprised you with your favorite meal. (R) (SL) (F)

Brainstorm ...

- What is the meal?
  - What are the ingredients?
  - What is the recipe?
  - How long did it take to make?
- What is your reaction?
- Is it any good?

Did you know?

In addition to our annual prompt anthologies, every year we have themed anthologies that you can also submit to!

You can find more information on our website, www.TCStudiosHQ.com.

#224 – It's fondue night! (S) (P) (SF)

Brainstorm ...

- Where are you going to get it?
- Does someone have a fondue machine?
- Who is coming?
- What food is going to be dipped?
- Is everyone bringing something?
  - What are you bringing?

Looking for a challenge?

Try doing one of our prompts with your friend(s)! See if you can come up with something together.

#225 – A la mode. (F) (H) (M)

Brainstorm …

- What is topped with ice cream?
- Is it hot or cold?
- What flavor is the ice cream?
- Is one or more person eating it?

Writing Exercise #45

Write about going apple picking on a date.

#226 – "Three second rule." (H) (SL) (D)

Brainstorm …

- What fell onto the floor?
- Who is about to eat it anyway?
- Is anyone watching?
    - How do they feel about it?
    - Would they do the same?

Did you know?

We also make books to help with storytelling. With help on things like creating characters, world-building, magic systems, and more!

You can find more information on our website,
www.TCStudiosHQ.com.

#227 – Someone has poisoned the buffet at a presidential speech. (R) (M) (AA)

> **Brainstorm …**
>
> - Why?
> - Who are they trying to kill?
>   - The President?
>   - The Vice President?
>   - Someone else?
> - How long does the poison take to kick in?
> - Are they going to get away with it?
> - What happens if they kill their target?
>   - What happens if they don't?

Did you know?

We also publish novels and comics that you can read!

You can find more information on our website,
www.TCStudiosHQ.com.

#228 – Lunch. (F) (P) (SL)

> *Brainstorm ...*
>
> - What's being served?
>   - Is it homemade?
>   - Who's making it?
>   - Is it fast food?
>   - How much does it cost?
> - Is it hot or cold?
> - Is there a drink being served with it?

Do you want to give us a prompt for next year's edition?

You can submit prompt ideas you have based on next year's chapter themes. Credit will be given if selected.

You can find more information on our website, www.TCStudiosHQ.com.

#229 – You've burnt it – again. (R) (SF) (S)

Brainstorm …

- What did you burn?
- How many times have you tried to make it?
- Who/what are you making it for?

Did you know?

We post daily writing & drawing prompts on our Social Medias for everyone to participate in.

Find us @PromptParty and use #PromptParty.

You can find more information on our website, www.TCStudiosHQ.com.

#230 – You're learning a new recipe. (SL) (H) (M)

Brainstorm ...

- What ingredients does it call for?
- What is the recipe like?
- Do you have all of the ingredients needed?
- Do you have all of the tools needed?
- How long does it take to make?

Writing Exercise #46

Write about cooking your favorite meal.

#231 – Chocolate-covered strawberries. (F) (R) (P)

Brainstorm …

- Why do you have them?
    - Just a snack?
    - Is it for something romantic?
- What kind of chocolate?
- Are they decorated in any way?

Did you know?

In addition to posting daily on Social Media, we have daily interactive posts on our YouTube channel, Podcast, and Blog.

You can find more information on our website, www.TCStudiosHQ.com.

#232 – You find a child going through your trash for food. (M) (S) (SL)

Brainstorm …

- What do they look like?
- Are they thin?
- Will you approach them?
  - Offer them food?
  - Bring them inside?
- Will you try to contact their parents?
- What will you do?

Remember!

The listed genres/mediums and brainstorming boxes are **only suggestions!** We encourage you to do/use whatever you want.

#233 – You've entered an eating contest. (SF) (H) (D)

> **Brainstorm …**
>
> - What food is the contest serving?
> - How are you preparing for the contest?
> - What's the prize for first place?
>   - Are there any other prizes?

Be The First To Know.

Join our newsletter and be the first to know about new prompt books, novels, comics, giveaways, freebies, coupons, and anything else we've got going on!

Find our newsletter on our website, www.TCStudiosHQ.com.

#234 – "I said tomatoes, not potatoes!" (SL) (R) (AA)

Brainstorm …

- Why do you need tomatoes?
- Is this going to ruin a meal?
- Is there still time to get tomatoes?
- What were/are you making?

You can share your work with us on Facebook, Instagram & Twitter!

Tag us @PromptParty and use #PromptParty.

We'd love to see what you come up with!

#235 – People start to go missing right around the time a new restaurant opens. (H) (M) (P)

Brainstorm ...

- Is there more to it than a coincidence?
- Who is going to find out?
  - You?
    - How?
      - What are you going to do?
      - Are you going to insist that the police investigate?
      - What if you're right, and they want to shut you up?

Writing Exercise #47

Write about going grocery shopping.

#236 – Something is burning … (AA) (F) (R)

Brainstorm …

- Where?
  - Your kitchen?
  - Someone else's kitchen?
- What's burning?
- Is it going to start a fire?
  - Has it already?
- Can it be stopped?
  - Should the fire department be called?

Do you want your work published?

You can submit any work made using our prompts to our annual anthologies! Published submissions receive shared 25% royalties.

You can find more information on our website,
www.TCStudiosHQ.com.

#237 – Your child is having an allergic reaction. (H) (SL) (SF)

Brainstorm ...

- To what?
- Do you have an EpiPen®?
- Do you have any Benadryl®?
- What are their symptoms?
- Is it severe?
- Should they be taken to the hospital?

Did you know?

A percentage of every anthology sold goes towards helping communities like yours. This includes donations to charities, funding of scholarships, creating of programs, and more!

You can find more information on our website, www.TCStudiosHQ.com.

#238 – Rats are nibbling away at a dead body you've come across in an alley. (H) (M) (D)

Brainstorm ...

- How much have they eaten?
- How many are there?
- Is it a man or woman?
- Have they been dead long?
- What are you going to do?

Did you know?

In addition to our annual prompt anthologies, every year we have themed anthologies that you can also submit to!

You can find more information on our website, www.TCStudiosHQ.com.

#239 – You're on the search for a rare fruit in the amazon. (AA) (F) (S)

Brainstorm ...

- Why are you searching for this fruit?
    - Does it have any interesting properties?
    - Is it worth a lot of money?
- How did you get to the amazon?
- Is there anyone else with you?

Looking for a challenge?

Try doing one of our prompts with your friend(s)! See if you can come up with something together.

#240 – Dinner. (SL) (P) (H)

Brainstorm …

- What's being served?
  - Is it homemade?
    - Who's making it?
  - Is it fast food?
    - How much does it cost?
- Is it hot or cold?
- Is there a drink being served with it?

Writing Exercise #48

Write about finding moldy food in your fridge.

#241 – Something smells good! (F) (R) (M)

Brainstorm ...

- Where are you?
- Where is the smell coming from?
- Can you find out what it is?
- Do you know who's cooking it?
- Are you going to get to eat it?

Did you know?

We also make books to help with storytelling. With help on things like creating characters, world-building, magic systems, and more!

You can find more information on our website, www.TCStudiosHQ.com.

#242 – You and your partner are out on a picnic. (R) (SL) (F)

Brainstorm …

- Where?
    - The park?
    - Your backyard?
- What kind of food did you bring?
    - Is it hot or cold?
- Did you bring anything else to do/eat?

Did you know?

We also publish novels and comics that you can read!

You can find more information on our website,
www.TCStudiosHQ.com.

#243 – You're so full you could pop. (SL) (S) (SF)

Brainstorm ...

- What did you eat?
- How good was it?
- What kind of food was it?
- Do you regret eating so much?
- Are you going to throw up?

Do you want to give us a prompt for next year's edition?

You can submit prompt ideas you have based on next year's chapter themes. Credit will be given if selected.

You can find more information on our website, www.TCStudiosHQ.com.

#244 – You're starving. (AA) (H) (D)

Brainstorm ...

- Literally?
- When was the last time you've eaten?
- Are you going to eat soon?
    - Are you able to?

Did you know?

We post daily writing & drawing prompts on our Social Medias for everyone to participate in.

Find us @PromptParty and use #PromptParty.

You can find more information on our website, www.TCStudiosHQ.com.

Chapter Nine: Magic.

#245 – You've just discovered your great grandfather was a necromancer. (F) (SF) (S)

Brainstorm ...

- Does anyone else in your family have magical abilities?
  - o Does it run in your family?
- Do you?
- Is your great grandfather alive?
- How did you find out he was/is a necromancer?
- What does/did he do with his power?

Writing Exercise #49

Creation a recipe for a potion.

#246 – When dusting off an old bottle in the attic, a genie emerges. (SL) (S) (R)

Brainstorm ...

- How did that bottle get up there?
- How long has it been there?
- Is the genie grateful or cranky?
- What are you going to wish for?

Did you know?

In addition to posting daily on Social Media, we have daily interactive posts on our YouTube channel, Podcast, and Blog.

You can find more information on our website, www.TCStudiosHQ.com.

#247 – You cast a spell with one intention – but something completely different happens. (H) (M) (P)

Brainstorm ...

- What was your original intention?
- What is happening instead?
- How did this happen?
- Was your wand/spell tampered with?
- Is there any way to fix it?
    - What if there isn't?
    - If there is, what might that be?

Remember!

The listed genres/mediums and brainstorming boxes are **only suggestions!** We encourage you to do/use whatever you want.

#248 – Your fiancé has been cursed. (S) (H) (R)

Brainstorm …

- By whom?
- What is the curse?
- How long does it last?
- How can it be broken?

Be The First To Know.

Join our newsletter and be the first to know about new prompt books, novels, comics, giveaways, freebies, coupons, and anything else we've got going on!

Find our newsletter on our website, www.TCStudiosHQ.com.

#249 – You are half human, half witch/wizard. (SL) (R) (F)

Brainstorm …

- Which of your parents is human, and which is magical?
- What is the extent of your power?
  - Can you control them yet?
- What is your daily life like?
- How do the mundane and magical worlds mix in your extended family?
  - Do they?
  - Do they not like each other?

You can share your work with us on Facebook, Instagram & Twitter!

Tag us @PromptParty and use #PromptParty.

We'd love to see what you come up with!

#250 – You're trying to learn some magic tricks. (F) (SL) (S)

> **Brainstorm ...**
>
> - What kind of magic tricks?
>   - What items do you need for them?
> - Are you getting them wrong or are you doing well?
> - Is anyone helping you?
> - How long have you been practicing to be a magician?

Writing Exercise #50

Write about a witch on the run.

#251 – A spell that was once keeping an evil overlord imprisoned has just been broken. (AA) (P) (F)

Brainstorm ...

- How was it broken?
    - Was there a time limit?
    - Did someone break it?
    - Did the overlord break it?
- What is the overlord going to do now?
- Is someone going to try to imprison them again?
    - How are they going to do that?
    - Can they?

Do you want your work published?

You can submit any work made using our prompts to our annual anthologies! Published submissions receive shared 25% royalties.

You can find more information on our website,
www.TCStudiosHQ.com.

#252 – "If we cast the spell together, we can take it down!" (AA) (D) (M)

Brainstorm …

- Who is we?
  - How many of them are there?
- What are they trying to take down?
- What kind of spell are they casting?
- What is going on here?

Did you know?

A percentage of every anthology sold goes towards helping communities like yours. This includes donations to charities, funding of scholarships, creating of programs, and more!

You can find more information on our website, www.TCStudiosHQ.com.

#253 – This spell enables you to inhabit someone's body for a day. (H) (R) (F)

Brainstorm ...

- Whose body do you want/need to inhabit?
  - Why?
- What are you going to do once you're in it?
- Is the person aware they are being controlled during this time?
- Do they have any memory of it afterwards?
- Can they break the spell while being controlled?

Did you know?

In addition to our annual prompt anthologies, every year we have themed anthologies that you can also submit to!

You can find more information on our website, www.TCStudiosHQ.com.

#254 – What happens when you accidently cast a curse? (H) (M) (S)

Brainstorm ...

- What spell were you trying to cast?
- What curse got cast instead?
- What or who is it effecting?
- How are you going to fix it?

Looking for a challenge?

Try doing one of our prompts with your friend(s)! See if you can come up with something together.

#255 – You're called on in the audience by a magician on stage. (F) (P) (SL)

Brainstorm …

- Are you willing to go up, or are you pressured to?
- What does the magician want you to do?
- How are you feeling?
  - Scared?
  - Excited?
  - Nervous?
- What does the magician do?

Writing Exercise #51

Write about a magic student's first day of class.

260

#256 – "Hurry up and cast the spell!" (AA) (F) (SF)

Brainstorm ...

- What spell do you need to cast?
- Why does it need to be done in a hurry?
- What happens once you cast it?
- What if you don't cast it in time?

Did you know?

We also make books to help with storytelling. With help on things like creating characters, world-building, magic systems, and more!

You can find more information on our website,
www.TCStudiosHQ.com.

#257 – You've been turned into a phoenix. (S) (M) (R)

Brainstorm ...

- How?
- By who or what?
- Is it a gradual or immediate process?
- What is your reaction?
- Is there a way to turn you back?
- Do you want to be turned back?
- Are you a full phoenix or a hybrid?

Did you know?

We also publish novels and comics that you can read!

You can find more information on our website,
www.TCStudiosHQ.com.

#258 – You're on the verge of creating a new magic system. (F) (SF) (S)

Brainstorm ...

- What kind of magic system?
- What are the rules?
- Are there restrictions?
- Are there consequences?
- Is there anyone else involved in creating this system?
  - Are you working well together or are you bumping heads?

Do you want to give us a prompt for next year's edition?

You can submit prompt ideas you have based on next year's chapter themes. Credit will be given if selected.

You can find more information on our website,
www.TCStudiosHQ.com.

#259 – A camera that creates 2D clones. (SF) (P) (S)

Brainstorm ...

- Are the clones functional?
- Do they have brains?
  - Do they think and act like the original?
- Is this only for inanimate objects?
  - If so, what would happen if it was used on a person?

Did you know?

We post daily writing & drawing prompts on our Social Medias for everyone to participate in.

Find us @PromptParty and use #PromptParty.

You can find more information on our website, www.TCStudiosHQ.com.

#260 – Fortune cookies actually tell fortunes. (SL) (R) (H)

Brainstorm ...

- How accurate are the fortunes?
- Can they be interpreted differently and still come true?
- What problems might this cause?
- Are these cookies able to change the string of fate?
- How do you go about getting these cookies?
  - Are they legal?
  - Are they sold on a black market?
  - How are they made?

Writing Exercise #52

Write about being cursed.

#261 – You are a master of the dark arts. (AA) (H) (S)

Brainstorm ...

- Do you use this power for good or evil?
- How did you become a master?
- Do you have any students?
- What kinds of items do you keep in your home/study?

Did you know?

In addition to posting daily on Social Media, we have daily interactive posts on our YouTube channel, Podcast, and Blog.

You can find more information on our website, www.TCStudiosHQ.com.

#262 – You cast the wrong spell and all hell breaks loose – literally. (S) (F) (H)

Brainstorm ...

- What spell did you cast?
- What did you mean to cast?
- What's happening now?
- Is there any way to correct or stop it?
- Will you face any consequences for casting such a dangerous spell?

Remember!

The listed genres/mediums and brainstorming boxes are **only suggestions!** We encourage you to do/use whatever you want.

#263 – Modern witch/wizard. (SL) (AA) (M)

Brainstorm ...

- What might one look like?
- How might one act?
- Is there a modern magic school they go to?
- Are they done with school?
- How do they use their magic?

Be The First To Know.

Join our newsletter and be the first to know about new prompt books, novels, comics, giveaways, freebies, coupons, and anything else we've got going on!

Find our newsletter on our website, www.TCStudiosHQ.com.

#264 – Teacher by day, witch hunter by night. (AA) (F) (S)

Brainstorm …

- What do they teach?
- Are they a respected teacher?
- Does anyone in the school know they hunt witches?
- Are they good at hunting?
- How many have they gotten?
- What is their process like?

You can share your work with us on Facebook, Instagram & Twitter!

Tag us @PromptParty and use #PromptParty.

We'd love to see what you come up with!

#265 – "Are you *trying* to hex me? Because, rude." (H) (R) (M)

Brainstorm ...

- *Are* they trying to hex them?
  - Why?
  - Are they upset with them?
  - Is it an accident?
  - What would the hex do?
- How can this person avoid being hexed?

Writing Exercise #53

Write about fighting an evil warlock.

#266 – A conversation with your reflection. (P) (S) (SL)

Brainstorm …

- What would you talk about?
- Which of you started the conversation?
  - ○ Were you expecting them to talk?
    - ▪ If not, what is your reaction?

Do you want your work published?

You can submit any work made using our prompts to our annual anthologies! Published submissions receive shared 25% royalties.

You can find more information on our website,
www.TCStudiosHQ.com.

#267 – You wear magic restraints to keep your power under control. (M) (F) (D)

Brainstorm …

- What do the restraints look like?
- Do you wear them willingly?
  - Are you forced to wear them?
    - Who controls them?
- What would happen if they came off?
  - Would it be worse for you or those around you?

Did you know?

A percentage of every anthology sold goes towards helping communities like yours. This includes donations to charities, funding of scholarships, creating of programs, and more!

You can find more information on our website, www.TCStudiosHQ.com.

#268 – "The book of forbidden spells … it's gone missing." (M) (AA) (S)

Brainstorm …

- Where was it?
- Was it being guarded?
- Who stole it?
    - Do we know?
- Have any forbidden spells been cast since it's gone missing?
    - How would we know?
- How are we going to get the book back?
    - Are we able to?
    - Can/should it be destroyed instead?

Did you know?

In addition to our annual prompt anthologies, every year we have <u>themed</u> anthologies that you can also submit to!

You can find more information on our website, www.TCStudiosHQ.com.

#269 – The ability to control shadows. (H) (S) (F)

Brainstorm ...

- What does it entail?
- Is there a cost?
- What would you do with the shadows?
- What happens to someone or something without their shadow?
- Is there a time limit?
- How many can be controlled at once?

Looking for a challenge?

Try doing one of our prompts with your friend(s)! See if you can come up with something together.

#270 – Each time a spell is cast, the planet grows closer to death. (H) (M) (SF)

Brainstorm ...

- Why?
    - ○ Is magic drawing energy from the planet?
    - ○ Is there a way to reverse this?
- Is magic outlawed because of this?
    - ○ Are people using it anyway?
- What state is the planet currently in?

Writing Exercise #54

Write about shopping for a wand.

#271 – The ability to manipulate the elements. (S) (F) (R)

> **Brainstorm …**
>
> - Is there a cost?
> - Can you manipulate more than one at a time?
> - What would you do with that power?
> - How is this power most commonly used?
> - Is there a tax on the planet when this is done?

Did you know?

We also make books to help with storytelling. With help on things like creating characters, world-building, magic systems, and more!

You can find more information on our website, www.TCStudiosHQ.com.

#272 – "Do you think we could get them to write that scroll for us?" (R) (S) (M)

Brainstorm ...

- What kind of scroll needs to be written?
- Who are they trying to get to write it?
- When do they need it?
- Would it cost them anything?
- What do they need the scroll for?
- What if they can't get it?

Did you know?

We also publish novels and comics that you can read!

You can find more information on our website,
www.TCStudiosHQ.com.

#273 – You've summoned the wrong mystical creature. (H) (AA) (D)

Brainstorm ...

- What were you trying to summon?
- What did you summon instead?
- Is it docile or hostile?
- What are you going to do with it?
- Are you still able to summon the other creature?

Do you want to give us a prompt for next year's edition?

You can submit prompt ideas you have based on next year's chapter themes. Credit will be given if selected.

You can find more information on our website, www.TCStudiosHQ.com.

#274 – All magic has been outlawed. (D) (AA) (M)

Brainstorm ...

- Why?
- Is it doing too much harm?
- How/When did it start?
- Are people rebelling against this law?

Did you know?

We post daily writing & drawing prompts on our Social Medias for everyone to participate in.

Find us @PromptParty and use #PromptParty.

You can find more information on our website, www.TCStudiosHQ.com.

#275 – You've been chosen to be your magic art school's successor. (SL) (S) (F)

Brainstorm …

- Why you?
- Do you accept this title?
- What are you going to do with this title?
    - Does this require any certain jobs or responsibilities?
- How do your friends/family feel about this?
- How do the other students feel about it?

Writing Exercise #55

Write about your powers being too strong for you to control.

Chapter Ten: Supernatural.

#276 – A werewolf has been reported lurking just outside your town. (S) (M) (H)

Brainstorm ...

- When did the sightings start?
- Has it hurt or killed anyone?
- Is it someone in town?
- Are they trying to get rid of it?
  - How?

Did you know?

In addition to posting daily on Social Media, we have daily interactive posts on our YouTube channel, Podcast, and Blog.

You can find more information on our website, www.TCStudiosHQ.com.

#277 – You spot someone using supernatural abilities – and they want you to keep quiet about it. (R) (SL) (D)

Brainstorm ...

- Where did you see them?
- What did you see them doing?
- Why do they want you to keep quiet about it?
- Are they threatening you so that you won't tell?
- Will you tell someone anyway?

Remember!

The listed genres/mediums and brainstorming boxes are **only suggestions!** We encourage you to do/use whatever you want.

#278 – You spot a mermaid while out fishing. (S) (SF) (AA)

Brainstorm ...

- Does it approach you or flee?
  - Will you go after it?
- What is it doing?
- What does it look like?
- Can it speak English?
- Are there any animals with it?

Be The First To Know.

Join our newsletter and be the first to know about new prompt books, novels, comics, giveaways, freebies, coupons, and anything else we've got going on!

Find our newsletter on our website, www.TCStudiosHQ.com.

#279 – After a hard hit to the head, you're starting to see supernatural creatures everywhere you look. (P) (H) (S)

Brainstorm …

- Are they docile or hostile?
- What are they doing?
- Can anyone else see them?
- Can you communicate with them?

You can share your work with us on Facebook, Instagram & Twitter!

Tag us @PromptParty and use #PromptParty.

We'd love to see what you come up with!

#280 – Vampires. (D) (SL) (R)

Brainstorm …

- Have you seen one?
- Were you attacked by one?
- Are you one?
- Are you trying to kill one?
- Do you know one?
- Are you in love with one?

Writing Exercise #56

Write about the process of becoming a vampire.

#281 – A device that allows you to read people's minds. (S) (M) (SF)

Brainstorm ...

- Who's mind would you want to read?
- What mischief would you cause with this device?
- What helpful acts would you do with this device?
- What could go wrong?
- What if it malfunctioned?

Do you want your work published?

You can submit any work made using our prompts to our annual anthologies! Published submissions receive shared 25% royalties.

You can find more information on our website, www.TCStudiosHQ.com.

#282 – People are starting to age backwards. (SF) (M) (R)

Brainstorm ...

- What is causing this?
- Is it magic?
- Is it some sort of illness?
- Can it be cured?

Did you know?

A percentage of every anthology sold goes towards helping communities like yours. This includes donations to charities, funding of scholarships, creating of programs, and more!

You can find more information on our website, www.TCStudiosHQ.com.

#283 – A nuclear explosion has started to give people strange abilities. (M) (AA) (D)

Brainstorm ...

- How long after the explosion are these abilities showing up?
- What are some of these abilities?
- How are people using them?
- Is the government concerned?
    - Are civilians?

Did you know?

In addition to our annual prompt anthologies, every year we have <u>themed</u> anthologies that you can also submit to!

You can find more information on our website, www.TCStudiosHQ.com.

#284 – The zombie apocalypse has begun. (S) (H) (D)

Brainstorm ...

- What started it?
  - Was it at random?
- Are you prepared?
- Do you know anyone who is?
- What are you going to do?
- Where are you going to go?
- Do you know any of the zombies?
- Have you seen anyone be attacked?
- Have you seen anyone turn into one?

Looking for a challenge?

Try doing one of our prompts with your friend(s)! See if you can come up with something together.

#285 – A new species of humans has started to emerge. (P) (R) (F)

Brainstorm ...

- What are they like?
- When did they start emerging?
  - Where did it start?
- What do they look like?
- Do they have any new/interesting traits?
- Are they blending in?
- Are they trying to rule over regular humans?
- What are they called?

Writing Exercise #57

Write about the process of becoming a werewolf.

#286 – Something is lurking in the shadows. (H) (S) (SF)

Brainstorm ...

- What could it be?
  - o   A person?
  - o   An animal?
  - o   A monster/demon?
- Where are you?
  - o   In the woods?
  - o   Inside?
- Are you going to figure out what is?
- Are you going to run away from it?

Did you know?

We also make books to help with storytelling. With help on things like creating characters, world-building, magic systems, and more!

You can find more information on our website,
www.TCStudiosHQ.com.

#287 – A cure is being researched for vampirism. (SF) (R) (SL)

Brainstorm …

- Who is researching it?
    - Humans?
    - Vampires?
    - Both?
- What does the research consist of?
- Are there any humans or vampires against it?
- How close are they to a cure?
    - Have they already found one?

Did you know?

We also publish novels and comics that you can read!

You can find more information on our website,
www.TCStudiosHQ.com.

#288 – Each zodiac sign is granted a set range of abilities. (F) (S) (D)

Brainstorm ...

- What kind of abilities?
- Are any of them against each other?
- Are any of them allies?
- Is there a divide between them?
- Do they all get along?
- How does this affect society?

Do you want to give us a prompt for next year's edition?

You can submit prompt ideas you have based on next year's chapter themes. Credit will be given if selected.

You can find more information on our website, www.TCStudiosHQ.com.

#289 – Their mission is to assassinate the king. (AA) (M) (SL)

Brainstorm …

- Who's mission?
- Why are they trying to kill the king?
- How many of them are there?
- What is their plan?
- Does the king know about their desire to kill him?
    - Is his security prepared?
- What happens if he dies?

Did you know?

We post daily writing & drawing prompts on our Social Medias for everyone to participate in.

Find us @PromptParty and use #PromptParty.

You can find more information on our website, www.TCStudiosHQ.com.

#290 – Mermaids are learning to live on land. (S) (F) (H)

Brainstorm …

- How are they doing this?
- Are people concerned?
- Are they able to hide among humans?
- Are they being chased off land, or being welcomed?
- How are they adjusting to life on land?

Writing Exercise #58

Write about the process of becoming a zombie.

#291 – Humans are being harvested to produce blood for vampires. (SF) (S) (H)

Brainstorm …

- How?
- Why?
  - o Are humans dying out?
- Are the humans rebelling?
  - o Are they donating willingly?
- When/how did this start?
- Is it a means to an end?

Did you know?

In addition to posting daily on Social Media, we have daily interactive posts on our YouTube channel, Podcast, and Blog.

You can find more information on our website, www.TCStudiosHQ.com.

#292 – Demons are walking among us. (SL) (H) (D)

Brainstorm ...

- Do they look like humans?
- Are they in their natural forms?
- How are we coexisting?
    - Is it going well?
    - Is it going poorly?
    - Are there any hybrid children?

Remember!

The listed genres/mediums and brainstorming boxes are **only suggestions!** We encourage you to do/use whatever you want.

#293 – Sirens are created when someone dies violently at sea. (AA) (H) (M)

Brainstorm …

- How long does it take?
  - Does it take a certain amount of time, or does the time vary?
- Does their death determine what they will look like?
- Do the sirens have any memory of being human?
  - Do they have any memory of their death?

Be The First To Know.

Join our newsletter and be the first to know about new prompt books, novels, comics, giveaways, freebies, coupons, and anything else we've got going on!

Find our newsletter on our website, www.TCStudiosHQ.com.

#294 – Humans have become nocturnal. (SF) (S) (P)

Brainstorm ...

- How did this happen?
- Are there any non-nocturnal humans left?
- How has this changed life for humans?
- What changes have been made because of this?

You can share your work with us on Facebook, Instagram & Twitter!

Tag us @PromptParty and use #PromptParty.

We'd love to see what you come up with!

#295 – The afterlife has a receptionist. (M) (S) (P)

Brainstorm ...

- What is their name?
- What is their personality like?
- Do they like they're job?
- How did they get this job?
    - Were they created for it?
    - Were they assigned to it?
- What does their day-to-day look like?
- What happens if they can't make it to work?

Writing Exercise #59

Write about traveling to the afterlife.

#296 – Monsters are flooding in from the sky. (H) (AA) (D)

Brainstorm ...

- Can they fly, or are they dropping in from some sort of portal?
- What are people's reactions?
- What are the monsters doing?
    - Are they destroying things?
    - Are they killing or kidnapping people?
- Is anyone doing anything to stop them?
    - Can they?

Do you want your work published?

You can submit any work made using our prompts to our annual anthologies! Published submissions receive shared 25% royalties.

You can find more information on our website,
www.TCStudiosHQ.com.

#297 – A woman has adopted Lucifer's child. (SL) (H) (S)

> **Brainstorm ...**
>
> - How did she find herself in this position?
> - What kind of child are they?
>   - Is it misbehaving?
>   - Is it well behaved?
> - How long will she have the child?
> - What are the terms or conditions?
> - What will happen if she abandons the child?

Did you know?

A percentage of every anthology sold goes towards helping communities like yours. This includes donations to charities, funding of scholarships, creating of programs, and more!

You can find more information on our website, www.TCStudiosHQ.com.

#298 – The ability to erase memories. (R) (S) (F)

> ### *Brainstorm …*
>
> - Who or what possesses this ability?
> - Is it being used for good or evil?
> - Are people grateful or resentful?
> - How long does it last?
>   - Is it permanent?

Did you know?

In addition to our annual prompt anthologies, every year we have themed anthologies that you can also submit to!

You can find more information on our website,
www.TCStudiosHQ.com.

#299 – The full moon's light is acidic. (SF) (S) (H)

Brainstorm ...

- How acidic is it?
- What is its effect on people? Plants? Animals? Water?
- Is there any way to combat it?
- Has it always been this way, or did it change?
  - If it changed, how or why did it?

Looking for a challenge?

Try doing one of our prompts with your friend(s)! See if you can come up with something together.

#300 – A cure is being researched for zombies. (SF) (H) (S)

Brainstorm ...

- When did zombies start appearing?
- Are they being kept in cages until the cure is found?
- Are there people wanting them gone instead?
- What does the research consist of?
    - Who is working on it?
- How far along is the cure?

Writing Exercise #60

Write about someone mastering their superpowers.

#301 – "Have you come for my soul?" (SL) (R) (P)

Brainstorm ...

- Who are they talking to?
    - Death?
    - The devil?
    - An angel?
- Have they come for their soul?
    - Have they come for something else?
        - If so, what could it be?
- What condition is this person in?
- Why do they think they're here for their soul?

Did you know?

We also make books to help with storytelling. With help on things like creating characters, world-building, magic systems, and more!

You can find more information on our website, www.TCStudiosHQ.com.

#302 – Your guardian angel hates you. (R) (SL) (S)

Brainstorm …

- Why?
- How does this effect your daily life?
- Do you know of your angel's existence?
- Can you talk to them?
- Can you try to make them like you more?

Did you know?

We also publish novels and comics that you can read!

You can find more information on our website,
www.TCStudiosHQ.com.

#303 – "The world's changed. It's best if you do, too." (D) (AA) (M)

Brainstorm ...

- How has the world changed?
- Why do you need to change as well?
  - ○ What happens if you do?
    - ▪ What would that process of change be like?
  - ○ What happens if you don't?
    - ▪ What would happen to you?

Do you want to give us a prompt for next year's edition?

You can submit prompt ideas you have based on next year's chapter themes. Credit will be given if selected.

You can find more information on our website, www.TCStudiosHQ.com.

#304 – A cure is being researched for werewolves. (M) (AA) (SF)

Brainstorm …

- When did werewolves start becoming a problem?
- Are they being kept in cages or separated in society until the cure is found?
- Are there people wanting them gone instead?
- What does the research consist of?
    - Who is working on it?
- How far along is the cure?

Did you know?

We post daily writing & drawing prompts on our Social Medias for everyone to participate in.

Find us @PromptParty and use #PromptParty.

You can find more information on our website, www.TCStudiosHQ.com.

#305 – You can have any wish granted – for a price. (H) (F) (S)

Brainstorm ...

- What is the price?
    - o   Is there a set price or does it adjust based on the wish?
- What would you wish for?
- How long will this opportunity last?
    - o   How did this opportunity appear?
- What if the wrong person got a hold of this?

Writing Exercise #61

Write about someone losing their superpowers.

Chapter Eleven: Villains.

#306 – "Impossible!" (AA) (S) (D)

Brainstorm ...

- What is?
- What's happening?
- Is someone defying the laws of physics?
- Has this villain laughably underestimated the situation?
- Is the *hero* saying this?

Did you know?

In addition to posting daily on Social Media, we have daily interactive posts on our YouTube channel, Podcast, and Blog.

You can find more information on our website, www.TCStudiosHQ.com.

#307 – Evil henchmen. (S) (M) (H)

Brainstorm ...

- Who do they work for?
- Where do they work?
- What kind of work do they do?
- Do they enjoy their work?
    - Are they looking for a way out?
- How did they become henchmen in the first place?
- How are they treated?

Remember!

The listed genres/mediums and brainstorming boxes are **only suggestions!** We encourage you to do/use whatever you want.

#308 – Infamous. (SL) (R) (P)

Brainstorm ...

- For what?
- How did they get this reputation?
- Are they proud of it?
- Are they ashamed of it?

Be The First To Know.

Join our newsletter and be the first to know about new prompt books, novels, comics, giveaways, freebies, coupons, and anything else we've got going on!

Find our newsletter on our website, www.TCStudiosHQ.com.

#309 – Someone has kidnapped you and is holding you hostage. (F) (AA) (H)

Brainstorm …

- Who is it?
    - Do you know the person?
    - Is it a stranger?
- What do they want?
- Are they trying to hurt someone else?
- Do they want money in exchange for you?
- Is there any way you can get away?

You can share your work with us on Facebook, Instagram & Twitter!

Tag us @PromptParty and use #PromptParty.

We'd love to see what you come up with!

#310 – You've taken an internship as an evil sidekick. (SL) (M) (S)

Brainstorm ...

- Why?
- What made you take this internship?
- Were you forced to?
- Do you want to be a villain some day?
- Whose sidekick are you?
- What does being their sidekick entail?

Writing Exercise #62

Write about a villain coming up with a plan.

#311 – World domination. (F) (SF) (D)

> *Brainstorm …*
>
> - Is someone trying to achieve it?
> - What would that involve?
> - Would it take more than one person?
> - Who would try to stop them?
>   - What if no one could?

Do you want your work published?

You can submit any work made using our prompts to our annual anthologies! Published submissions receive shared 25% royalties.

You can find more information on our website, www.TCStudiosHQ.com.

#312 – "You'll never stop me!" (D) (AA) (M)

Brainstorm ...

- What are they trying to do?
- Who is trying to stop them?
- What happens once they do?
- What happens if they can't?

Did you know?

A percentage of every anthology sold goes towards helping communities like yours. This includes donations to charities, funding of scholarships, creating of programs, and more!

You can find more information on our website, www.TCStudiosHQ.com.

#313 – A villain has placed several bombs throughout your city. (H) (SF) (M)

Brainstorm …

- Why?
- What are they trying to accomplish?
- Where are they placed?
  - Are they hidden?
- Are people out looking for them?
- Do the authorities know that they're around?
- What can you do to stop the villain from detonating them?

Did you know?

In addition to our annual prompt anthologies, every year we have themed anthologies that you can also submit to!

You can find more information on our website, www.TCStudiosHQ.com.

#314 – Your best friend has decided to join the bad guys. (R) (F) (S)

Brainstorm …

- Why?
- What led them to this decision?
  - Are they being forced?
  - Are they doing it for your sake?
  - Do they genuinely want to join them?
- What if they aren't the bad guys?
- Are you going to try to get them back?

Looking for a challenge?

Try doing one of our prompts with your friend(s)! See if you can
come up with something together.

#315 – A villain posing as a damsel in distress. (H) (AA) (D)

Brainstorm ...

- What are they doing?
- How are they pretending to be in danger?
- Who was tricked into trying to save them?
- What happens when it's revealed to be a trap?

Writing Exercise #63

Write about the application process of an evil henchmen.

#316 – Rotten to the core. (P) (S) (H)

Brainstorm ...

- How can this be interpreted?
- Who or what is being talked about?

Did you know?

We also make books to help with storytelling. With help on things like creating characters, world-building, magic systems, and more!

You can find more information on our website,
www.TCStudiosHQ.com.

#317 – A retired villain now serving as an advisor to heroes. (SL) (AA) (D)

Brainstorm …

- How and when did this happen?
- Are they getting anything in return?
- How have they helped the heroes?
- Are they skeptical of them?

Did you know?

We also publish novels and comics that you can read!

You can find more information on our website, www.TCStudiosHQ.com.

#318 – Severed limbs are showing up on people's doorsteps. (H) (M) (P)

Brainstorm ...

- Are they specific people's homes?
  - o   Are they parts of their families?
- Who is doing this?
- Is it more than one person?
- Is anyone trying to stop them?
- Have they made any progress?

Do you want to give us a prompt for next year's edition?

You can submit prompt ideas you have based on next year's chapter themes. Credit will be given if selected.

You can find more information on our website, www.TCStudiosHQ.com.

#319 – Evil lair. (AA) (SL) (S)

Brainstorm ...

- What does it look like?
- Who does it belong to?
- How big is it?
- Does it look like something else on the outside?
- What's in it?
- Has anyone found it?

Did you know?

We post daily writing & drawing prompts on our Social Medias for everyone to participate in.

Find us @PromptParty and use #PromptParty.

You can find more information on our website, www.TCStudiosHQ.com.

#320 – "Must you ruin everything?" (F) (SF) (R)

> ### *Brainstorm ...*
>
> - Who are they talking to?
> - What are they doing to ruin something?
> - What are they ruining?
> - Is it their fault?
> - Can it be helped?

Writing Exercise #64

Write about your life as a villain.

#321 – Every villain is a hero in their own mind. (SL) (F) (S)

Brainstorm ...

- What might be some examples?
- How might their judgement be skewed?
- How might you change their mind?
  - Can it be changed?

Did you know?

In addition to posting daily on Social Media, we have daily interactive posts on our YouTube channel, Podcast, and Blog.

You can find more information on our website, www.TCStudiosHQ.com.

#322 – Someone forced to be evil. (M) (P) (D)

Brainstorm ...

- How might this happen?
    - o Are they becoming evil to save someone else?
    - o Are they being bribed somehow?
    - o Have they been cursed?

Remember!

The listed genres/mediums and brainstorming boxes are **only suggestions!** We encourage you to do/use whatever you want.

#323 – "I'd always wanted to be a hero … Funny how the world works."
(R) (F) (SL)

Brainstorm …

- What happened to make this person a villain?
- How long did they try to be a hero?
  - What were they doing?
- Is there any way to change their mind?
- Is this person spiteful?
  - What could the tone be of this statement?

Be The First To Know.

Join our newsletter and be the first to know about new prompt books, novels, comics, giveaways, freebies, coupons, and anything else we've got going on!

Find our newsletter on our website, www.TCStudiosHQ.com.

#324 – You've fallen for the villain. (R) (AA) (S)

Brainstorm ...

- Who are they?
- Did you know them before they were evil?
  - Did you meet them as a villain?
- What's making you fall for them?
- Is anyone trying to change your mind?
- Is anyone trying to take them down?
- How do they feel about you?

You can share your work with us on Facebook, Instagram & Twitter!

Tag us @PromptParty and use #PromptParty.

We'd love to see what you come up with!

#325 – "I'm going to burn this world to the ground." (H) (P) (SF)

Brainstorm ...

- Is this being said literally or figuratively?
  - How would they do this either way?
  - What would their plan be?
- Would they have help?
- Who would try to stop them?
  - Could they?

Writing Exercise #65

Write about your life as a hero.

#326 – A hero undercover as a villain. (AA) (M) (D)

Brainstorm ...

- What would they have to do?
- What would they look like?
- What would their name be?
- Who would be in on it?
- What would they have to do?
  - Why are they doing this in the first place?
- What would happen if they got caught?

Do you want your work published?

You can submit any work made using our prompts to our annual anthologies! Published submissions receive shared 25% royalties.

You can find more information on our website,
www.TCStudiosHQ.com.

#327 – A villain's costume. (SF) (S) (SL)

> **Brainstorm ...**
>
> - What would one look like?
> - Would there be a cape?
> - What materials would it use?
> - Would it have any abilities or features built in?
> - Is it easy or hard to get on and off?

Did you know?

A percentage of every anthology sold goes towards helping communities like yours. This includes donations to charities, funding of scholarships, creating of programs, and more!

You can find more information on our website, www.TCStudiosHQ.com.

#328 – An adult villain can't bring themselves to fight an underaged hero. (F) (AA) (M)

Brainstorm …

- Why not?
- Do they know them?
- Do they like children?
  - Do they think they're innocent?
- What happens if they can't fight them?
  - Will the villain be captured or killed?
- Will the kid back down as well?
  - Will a different villain fight them instead?

Did you know?

In addition to our annual prompt anthologies, every year we have themed anthologies that you can also submit to!

You can find more information on our website, www.TCStudiosHQ.com.

#329 – "You're letting me go? Aren't you the bad guy?" (R) (H) (P)

Brainstorm …

- Who are they letting go?
  - Was it a hostage?
  - Was it a hero?
- Why?
  - Have they changed their mind about their plan?
  - Have they fallen for this person?
  - Are they being forced to?
- What happens if other villains find out?
- What will the escaped person do now?

Looking for a challenge?

Try doing one of our prompts with your friend(s)! See if you can come up with something together.

#330 – "Who's ready to get in a little trouble?" (D) (S) (SL)

Brainstorm ...

- Who is asking the question?
    - A villain?
    - An anti-hero?
    - Some teenager?
- What kind of trouble are they talking about?
- Will they actually get in trouble?
    - What if they do?
    - Do they have an exit/a backup plan?

Writing Exercise #66

Write about the life of a villain's child.

335

#331 – Someone thought to be a villain is actually a hero. (M) (S) (AA)

Brainstorm ...

- How could this mistake be made?
  - What might they have been doing?
  - Who might they have been associating with?
  - Were they forced to dress/act like one?
    - Were they undercover?
- What did they do to get people to see they were a villain?

Did you know?

We also make books to help with storytelling. With help on things like creating characters, world-building, magic systems, and more!

You can find more information on our website, www.TCStudiosHQ.com.

#332 – Notorious. (F) (SF) (H)

Brainstorm …

- For what?
- Who is that determined by?
- Who is it referring to?

Did you know?

We also publish novels and comics that you can read!

You can find more information on our website,
www.TCStudiosHQ.com.

#333 – "The hero life's never done anything for me." (SL) (R) (M)

Brainstorm ...

- How long has this person been a hero?
    o Are they?
- Why would they say this?
- Have they had bad luck trying to be a hero?
- Can someone prove them wrong?
- Are they thinking of becoming a villain instead?

Do you want to give us a prompt for next year's edition?

You can submit prompt ideas you have based on next year's chapter themes. Credit will be given if selected.

You can find more information on our website, www.TCStudiosHQ.com.

#334 – A villain driven by logic. (SF) (S) (H)

Brainstorm ...

- What might they do?
- How might they act?
- How might heroes/villains react to them?
- Is their thought process working for them?
    - Is it not?

Did you know?

We post daily writing & drawing prompts on our Social Medias for everyone to participate in.

Find us @PromptParty and use #PromptParty.

You can find more information on our website, www.TCStudiosHQ.com.

#335 – A villain driven by emotion. (F) (R) (P)

Brainstorm …

- What might they do?
- How might they act?
- How might heroes/villains react to them?
- Is their thought process working for them?
  - Is it not?

Writing Exercise #67

Write about a hero who is becoming a villain.

#336 – The villain realizes they're wrong. (M) (AA) (D)

Brainstorm ...

- How did they come to this realization?
  - Did someone show/tell them?
- What are they going to do now?

Did you know?

In addition to posting daily on Social Media, we have daily interactive posts on our YouTube channel, Podcast, and Blog.

You can find more information on our website, www.TCStudiosHQ.com.

Chapter Twelve: Words.

#337 – Crossbow. (AA) (H) (F)

Brainstorm ...

- What kinds of context could this word be used in?
  - Suspenseful?
  - Intimate?
  - Stressful?
  - Comical?
  - Mundane?
- What might be the situation surrounding this word be like?
- Try adding the next word that comes to mind when thinking of this one.
- Does this word have to be the main focus?
  - Can it support the scene instead?
  - Maybe it's only mentioned in passing.

Remember!

The listed genres/mediums and brainstorming boxes are **only suggestions!** We encourage you to do/use whatever you want.

#338 – Extension. (SL) (SF) (S)

Brainstorm …

- What kinds of context could this word be used in?
  - Suspenseful?
  - Intimate?
  - Stressful?
  - Comical?
  - Mundane?
- What might be the situation surrounding this word be like?
- Try adding the next word that comes to mind when thinking of this one.
- Does this word have to be the main focus?
  - Can it support the scene instead?
  - Maybe it's only mentioned in passing.

Be The First To Know.

Join our newsletter and be the first to know about new prompt books, novels, comics, giveaways, freebies, coupons, and anything else we've got going on!

Find our newsletter on our website, www.TCStudiosHQ.com.

#339 – Laptop. (SF) (P) (M)

Brainstorm …

- What kinds of context could this word be used in?
    - Suspenseful?
    - Intimate?
    - Stressful?
    - Comical?
    - Mundane?
- What might be the situation surrounding this word be like?
- Try adding the next word that comes to mind when thinking of this one.
- Does this word have to be the main focus?
    - Can it support the scene instead?
    - Maybe it's only mentioned in passing.

You can share your work with us on Facebook, Instagram & Twitter!

Tag us @PromptParty and use #PromptParty.

We'd love to see what you come up with!

#340 – Fleece. (SL) (D) (R)

Brainstorm …

- What kinds of context could this word be used in?
    - Suspenseful?
    - Intimate?
    - Stressful?
    - Comical?
    - Mundane?
- What might be the situation surrounding this word be like?
- Try adding the next word that comes to mind when thinking of this one.
- Does this word have to be the main focus?
    - Can it support the scene instead?
    - Maybe it's only mentioned in passing.

Writing Exercise #68

Write a scene based around your favorite word.

345

#341 – DVD. (R) (F) (M)

Brainstorm …

- What kinds of context could this word be used in?
  - Suspenseful?
  - Intimate?
  - Stressful?
  - Comical?
  - Mundane?
- What might be the situation surrounding this word be like?
- Try adding the next word that comes to mind when thinking of this one.
- Does this word have to be the main focus?
  - Can it support the scene instead?
  - Maybe it's only mentioned in passing.

Do you want your work published?

You can submit any work made using our prompts to our annual anthologies! Published submissions receive shared 25% royalties.

You can find more information on our website, www.TCStudiosHQ.com.

#342 – Stationary. (SF) (AA) (P)

Brainstorm ...

- What kinds of context could this word be used in?
  - Suspenseful?
  - Intimate?
  - Stressful?
  - Comical?
  - Mundane?
- What might be the situation surrounding this word be like?
- Try adding the next word that comes to mind when thinking of this one.
- Does this word have to be the main focus?
  - Can it support the scene instead?
  - Maybe it's only mentioned in passing.

Did you know?

A percentage of every anthology sold goes towards helping communities like yours. This includes donations to charities, funding of scholarships, creating of programs, and more!

You can find more information on our website, www.TCStudiosHQ.com.

#343 – Void. (P) (S) (H)

Brainstorm …

- What kinds of context could this word be used in?
    - Suspenseful?
    - Intimate?
    - Stressful?
    - Comical?
    - Mundane?
- What might be the situation surrounding this word be like?
- Try adding the next word that comes to mind when thinking of this one.
- Does this word have to be the main focus?
    - Can it support the scene instead?
    - Maybe it's only mentioned in passing.

Did you know?

In addition to our annual prompt anthologies, every year we have themed anthologies that you can also submit to!

You can find more information on our website, www.TCStudiosHQ.com.

#344 – Tunnel. (H) (AA) (M)

Brainstorm …

- What kinds of context could this word be used in?
  - Suspenseful?
  - Intimate?
  - Stressful?
  - Comical?
  - Mundane?
- What might be the situation surrounding this word be like?
- Try adding the next word that comes to mind when thinking of this one.
- Does this word have to be the main focus?
  - Can it support the scene instead?
  - Maybe it's only mentioned in passing.

Looking for a challenge?

Try doing one of our prompts with your friend(s)! See if you can come up with something together.

#345 – Burp. (SL) (F) (S)

Brainstorm …

- What kinds of context could this word be used in?
  - Suspenseful?
  - Intimate?
  - Stressful?
  - Comical?
  - Mundane?
- What might be the situation surrounding this word be like?
- Try adding the next word that comes to mind when thinking of this one.
- Does this word have to be the main focus?
  - Can it support the scene instead?
  - Maybe it's only mentioned in passing.

Writing Exercise #69

Create three words out of your first and last name, then write a scene using them.

#346 – Chair. (R) (D) (P)

Brainstorm …

- What kinds of context could this word be used in?
    - Suspenseful?
    - Intimate?
    - Stressful?
    - Comical?
    - Mundane?
- What might be the situation surrounding this word be like?
- Try adding the next word that comes to mind when thinking of this one.
- Does this word have to be the main focus?
    - Can it support the scene instead?
    - Maybe it's only mentioned in passing.

Did you know?

We also make books to help with storytelling. With help on things like creating characters, world-building, magic systems, and more!

You can find more information on our website, www.TCStudiosHQ.com.

#347 – Deer. (M) (AA) (F)

Brainstorm …

- What kinds of context could this word be used in?
    - Suspenseful?
    - Intimate?
    - Stressful?
    - Comical?
    - Mundane?
- What might be the situation surrounding this word be like?
- Try adding the next word that comes to mind when thinking of this one.
- Does this word have to be the main focus?
    - Can it support the scene instead?
    - Maybe it's only mentioned in passing.

Did you know?

We also publish novels and comics that you can read!

You can find more information on our website, www.TCStudiosHQ.com.

#348 – Fire. (F) (SF) (R)

Brainstorm …

- What kinds of context could this word be used in?
    - Suspenseful?
    - Intimate?
    - Stressful?
    - Comical?
    - Mundane?
- What might be the situation surrounding this word be like?
- Try adding the next word that comes to mind when thinking of this one.
- Does this word have to be the main focus?
    - Can it support the scene instead?
    - Maybe it's only mentioned in passing.

Do you want to give us a prompt for next year's edition?

You can submit prompt ideas you have based on next year's chapter themes. Credit will be given if selected.

You can find more information on our website,
www.TCStudiosHQ.com.

#349 – Steps. (SL) (D) (S)

Brainstorm …

- What kinds of context could this word be used in?
    - Suspenseful?
    - Intimate?
    - Stressful?
    - Comical?
    - Mundane?
- What might be the situation surrounding this word be like?
- Try adding the next word that comes to mind when thinking of this one.
- Does this word have to be the main focus?
    - Can it support the scene instead?
    - Maybe it's only mentioned in passing.

Did you know?

We post daily writing & drawing prompts on our Social Medias for everyone to participate in.

Find us @PromptParty and use #PromptParty.

You can find more information on our website, www.TCStudiosHQ.com.

#350 – Plant. (AA) (SF) (H)

Brainstorm ...

- What kinds of context could this word be used in?
  - Suspenseful?
  - Intimate?
  - Stressful?
  - Comical?
  - Mundane?
- What might be the situation surrounding this word be like?
- Try adding the next word that comes to mind when thinking of this one.
- Does this word have to be the main focus?
  - Can it support the scene instead?
  - Maybe it's only mentioned in passing.

Writing Exercise #70

Write a scene based on your least favorite word.

#351 – Frame. (M) (S) (F)

Brainstorm …

- What kinds of context could this word be used in?
    - Suspenseful?
    - Intimate?
    - Stressful?
    - Comical?
    - Mundane?
- What might be the situation surrounding this word be like?
- Try adding the next word that comes to mind when thinking of this one.
- Does this word have to be the main focus?
    - Can it support the scene instead?
    - Maybe it's only mentioned in passing.

Did you know?

In addition to posting daily on Social Media, we have daily interactive posts on our YouTube channel, Podcast, and Blog.

You can find more information on our website, www.TCStudiosHQ.com.

#352 – Plush. (P) (SL) (R)

Brainstorm …

- What kinds of context could this word be used in?
  - Suspenseful?
  - Intimate?
  - Stressful?
  - Comical?
  - Mundane?
- What might be the situation surrounding this word be like?
- Try adding the next word that comes to mind when thinking of this one.
- Does this word have to be the main focus?
  - Can it support the scene instead?
  - Maybe it's only mentioned in passing.

Remember!

The listed genres/mediums and brainstorming boxes are **only suggestions!** We encourage you to do/use whatever you want.

#353 – Decline. (R) (H) (AA)

Brainstorm …

- What kinds of context could this word be used in?
  - Suspenseful?
  - Intimate?
  - Stressful?
  - Comical?
  - Mundane?
- What might be the situation surrounding this word be like?
- Try adding the next word that comes to mind when thinking of this one.
- Does this word have to be the main focus?
  - Can it support the scene instead?
  - Maybe it's only mentioned in passing.

Be The First To Know.

Join our newsletter and be the first to know about new prompt books, novels, comics, giveaways, freebies, coupons, and anything else we've got going on!

Find our newsletter on our website, www.TCStudiosHQ.com.

#354 – Gold. (AA) (S) (F)

Brainstorm …

- What kinds of context could this word be used in?
  - Suspenseful?
  - Intimate?
  - Stressful?
  - Comical?
  - Mundane?
- What might be the situation surrounding this word be like?
- Try adding the next word that comes to mind when thinking of this one.
- Does this word have to be the main focus?
  - Can it support the scene instead?
  - Maybe it's only mentioned in passing.

You can share your work with us on Facebook, Instagram & Twitter!

Tag us @PromptParty and use #PromptParty.

We'd love to see what you come up with!

#355 – Bubble. (SF) (M) (D)

Brainstorm …

- What kinds of context could this word be used in?
    - Suspenseful?
    - Intimate?
    - Stressful?
    - Comical?
    - Mundane?
- What might be the situation surrounding this word be like?
- Try adding the next word that comes to mind when thinking of this one.
- Does this word have to be the main focus?
    - Can it support the scene instead?
    - Maybe it's only mentioned in passing.

Writing Exercise #71

Pick three words that describe your life, then write a scene based on them.

#356 – Box. (R) (H) (SL)

Brainstorm ...

- What kinds of context could this word be used in?
    - Suspenseful?
    - Intimate?
    - Stressful?
    - Comical?
    - Mundane?
- What might be the situation surrounding this word be like?
- Try adding the next word that comes to mind when thinking of this one.
- Does this word have to be the main focus?
    - Can it support the scene instead?
    - Maybe it's only mentioned in passing.

Do you want your work published?

You can submit any work made using our prompts to our annual anthologies! Published submissions receive shared 25% royalties.

You can find more information on our website, www.TCStudiosHQ.com.

#357 – Grind. (F) (AA) (P)

Brainstorm …

- What kinds of context could this word be used in?
  - Suspenseful?
  - Intimate?
  - Stressful?
  - Comical?
  - Mundane?
- What might be the situation surrounding this word be like?
- Try adding the next word that comes to mind when thinking of this one.
- Does this word have to be the main focus?
  - Can it support the scene instead?
  - Maybe it's only mentioned in passing.

Did you know?

A percentage of every anthology sold goes towards helping communities like yours. This includes donations to charities, funding of scholarships, creating of programs, and more!

You can find more information on our website, www.TCStudiosHQ.com.

#358 – Curtain. (P) (H) (SL)

Brainstorm …

- What kinds of context could this word be used in?
    o Suspenseful?
    o Intimate?
    o Stressful?
    o Comical?
    o Mundane?
- What might be the situation surrounding this word be like?
- Try adding the next word that comes to mind when thinking of this one.
- Does this word have to be the main focus?
    o Can it support the scene instead?
    o Maybe it's only mentioned in passing.

Did you know?

In addition to our annual prompt anthologies, every year we have
themed anthologies that you can also submit to!

You can find more information on our website,
www.TCStudiosHQ.com.

\#359 – Switch. (R) (M) (D)

Brainstorm …

- What kinds of context could this word be used in?
  - Suspenseful?
  - Intimate?
  - Stressful?
  - Comical?
  - Mundane?
- What might be the situation surrounding this word be like?
- Try adding the next word that comes to mind when thinking of this one.
- Does this word have to be the main focus?
  - Can it support the scene instead?
  - Maybe it's only mentioned in passing.

Looking for a challenge?

Try doing one of our prompts with your friend(s)! See if you can come up with something together.

#360 – Number. (SL) (R) (SF)

Brainstorm ...

- What kinds of context could this word be used in?
    o Suspenseful?
    o Intimate?
    o Stressful?
    o Comical?
    o Mundane?
- What might be the situation surrounding this word be like?
- Try adding the next word that comes to mind when thinking of this one.
- Does this word have to be the main focus?
    o Can it support the scene instead?
    o Maybe it's only mentioned in passing.

Writing Exercise #72

Take the first and last word of your favorite book, then write a scene using them.

365

#361 – Stage. (AA) (SL) (H)

Brainstorm ...

- What kinds of context could this word be used in?
  - Suspenseful?
  - Intimate?
  - Stressful?
  - Comical?
  - Mundane?
- What might be the situation surrounding this word be like?
- Try adding the next word that comes to mind when thinking of this one.
- Does this word have to be the main focus?
  - Can it support the scene instead?
  - Maybe it's only mentioned in passing.

Did you know?

We also make books to help with storytelling. With help on things like creating characters, world-building, magic systems, and more!

You can find more information on our website, www.TCStudiosHQ.com.

#362 – Show. (SL) (S) (D)

Brainstorm ...

- What kinds of context could this word be used in?
  - Suspenseful?
  - Intimate?
  - Stressful?
  - Comical?
  - Mundane?
- What might be the situation surrounding this word be like?
- Try adding the next word that comes to mind when thinking of this one.
- Does this word have to be the main focus?
  - Can it support the scene instead?
  - Maybe it's only mentioned in passing.

Did you know?

We also publish novels and comics that you can read!

You can find more information on our website,
www.TCStudiosHQ.com.

#363 – Sun. (D) (F) (AA)

Brainstorm …

- What kinds of context could this word be used in?
    - Suspenseful?
    - Intimate?
    - Stressful?
    - Comical?
    - Mundane?
- What might be the situation surrounding this word be like?
- Try adding the next word that comes to mind when thinking of this one.
- Does this word have to be the main focus?
    - Can it support the scene instead?
    - Maybe it's only mentioned in passing.

Do you want to give us a prompt for next year's edition?

You can submit prompt ideas you have based on next year's chapter themes. Credit will be given if selected.

You can find more information on our website,
www.TCStudiosHQ.com.

#364 – Fly. (AA) (P) (SF)

Brainstorm ...

- What kinds of context could this word be used in?
  - Suspenseful?
  - Intimate?
  - Stressful?
  - Comical?
  - Mundane?
- What might be the situation surrounding this word be like?
- Try adding the next word that comes to mind when thinking of this one.
- Does this word have to be the main focus?
  - Can it support the scene instead?
  - Maybe it's only mentioned in passing.

Did you know?

We post daily writing & drawing prompts on our Social Medias for everyone to participate in.

Find us @PromptParty and use #PromptParty.

You can find more information on our website, www.TCStudiosHQ.com.

#365 – Board. (SL) (M) (H)

Brainstorm …

- What kinds of context could this word be used in?
    - Suspenseful?
    - Intimate?
    - Stressful?
    - Comical?
    - Mundane?
- What might be the situation surrounding this word be like?
- Try adding the next word that comes to mind when thinking of this one.
- Does this word have to be the main focus?
    - Can it support the scene instead?
    - Maybe it's only mentioned in passing.

Writing Exercise #73

Take the first and last word of your favorite song, then write a scene using them.

Prompts By Genre

Fantasy (F)

1. #7 – You've been given a treasure map by a homeless man.
2. #9 – You've been hired as a private investigator.
3. #16 – You're a pirate preparing to set sail.
4. #27 – You just discovered you've got extraordinary powers.
5. #37 – "Any second now."
6. #43 – You're tired of waiting. It's time to take action.
7. #46 – It starts at midnight. Hope you're ready.
8. #48 – Your spell will only last for two minutes.
9. #53 – The ability to stop time.
10. #56 – "There's no time! Go!"
11. #57 – The dragons soar through the skies every night at dusk.
12. #60 – You're face to face with Father Time.
13. #62 – The ability to speak to and understand animals.
14. #63 – You are a crossbreed between a human and a mystical creature.
15. #66 – You're a dragon tamer.
16. #72 – There's something growling out there in the darkness.
17. #74 – An animal that can speak English.
18. #84 – There's something aboard your ship – and it's hungry.
19. #91 – You find a wild horse nursing a unicorn.
20. #98 – An injector is pumping poison into the Earth.
21. #103 – You're in a toy store when all of the remote-controlled cars start heading towards you.
22. #110 – You're working on something that could win your side the war.
23. #114 – You find a foreign piece of technology. It almost seems … alien.
24. #119 – "We didn't have this back in my day."
25. #126 – "… Where are we?"
26. #127 – You're on an alien planet – with no way to get back home.
27. #133 – Road trip!
28. #136 – Go to your happy place. They won't find you there.
29. #137 – Were you just … teleported?

30. #140 – Someone offers to take you to a magical place. Will you go?
31. #144 – "This isn't the time or the place for that."
32. #147 – So this is what heaven look like.
33. #148 – So this is what hell looks like.
34. #150 – You've got the map – now you just need someone who can read it.
35. #159 – Some kids in your neighbor's garage may or may not have just successfully created a teleportation machine.
36. #162 – The world's greatest scientists have banded together to take over the world.
37. #163 – Your scientific experiment is about to go horribly, horribly wrong.
38. #165 – Aliens have agreed to share their scientific knowledge with us.
39. #174 – What would your field of research be if you were a scientist?
40. #178 – A device that lets you slow or quick your eyes frame rate.
41. #184 – Rage.
42. #186 – Love.
43. #188 – Sorrow.
44. #193 – Curiosity.
45. #196 – Fatigue.
46. #197 – Frustration.
47. #198 – Hope.
48. #199 – Lust.
49. #204 – Worry.
50. #207 – Flirtatious.
51. #211 – Submissive.
52. #215 – Breakfast.
53. #217 – "This is delicious!"
54. #220 – You start as a waitress tomorrow night.
55. #223 – Your partner has surprised you with your favorite meal.
56. #225 – A la mode.
57. #228 – Lunch.
58. #231 – Chocolate-covered strawberries.
59. #236 – Something is burning …
60. #239 – You're on the search for a rare fruit in the amazon.
61. #241 – Something smells good!
62. #242 – You and your partner are out on a picnic.

63. #245 – You've just discovered your great grandfather was a necromancer.
64. #249 – You are half human, half witch/wizard.
65. #250 – You're trying to learn some magic tricks.
66. #251 – A spell that was once keeping an evil overlord imprisoned has just been broken.
67. #253 – This spell enables you to inhabit someone's body for a day.
68. #255 – You're called on in the audience by a magician on stage.
69. #256 – "Hurry up and cast the spell!"
70. #258 – You're on the verge of creating a new magic system.
71. #262 – You cast the wrong spell and all hell breaks loose – literally.
72. #264 – Teacher by day, witch hunter by night.
73. #267 – You wear magic restraints to keep your power under control.
74. #269 – The ability to control shadows.
75. #271 – The ability to manipulate the elements.
76. #275 – You've been chosen to be your magic art school's successor.
77. #285 – A new species of humans has started to emerge.
78. #288 – Each zodiac sign is granted a set range of abilities.
79. #290 – Mermaids are learning to live on land.
80. #298 – The ability to erase memories.
81. #305 – You can have any wish granted – for a price.
82. #309 – Someone has kidnapped you and is holding you hostage.
83. #311 – World domination.
84. #314 – Your best friend has decided to join the bad guys.
85. #320 – "Must you ruin everything?"
86. #321 – Every villain is a hero in their own mind.
87. #323 – "I'd always wanted to be a hero … Funny how the world works."
88. #328 – An adult villain can't bring themselves to fight an underaged hero.
89. #332 – Notorious.
90. #335 – A villain driven by emotion.
91. #337 – Crossbow.
92. #341 – DVD.
93. #345 – Burp.
94. #347 – Deer.

95. #348 – Fire.
96. #351 – Frame.
97. #354 – Gold.
98. #357 – Grind.
99. #363 – Sun.

Science Fiction (SF)

1. #2 – You run into yourself in a dream, but something isn't right – they're trying their hardest to stay away from you.
2. #8 – You've just found out that your best friend is an alien.
3. #18 – You're about to meet an author who has changed your life.
4. #27 – You just discovered you've got extraordinary powers.
5. #30 – "You'll pay for this!"
6. #31 – You regret your decision.
7. #33 – There's a ticking time-bomb. Red wire, or blue?
8. #34 – You wake up 100 years into the future.
9. #35 – You wake up 100 years into the past.
10. #42 – The only way to save the future, is to destroy the past.
11. #44 – You've got one minute to sever your arm, or you'll die.
12. #45 – All of the clocks in your home have stopped.
13. #47 – "What a time to be alive."
14. #50 – "Good timing."
15. #51 – If you had the ability to see your future, would you?
16. #52 – If you could change one thing from your past, what would it be?
17. #53 – The ability to stop time.
18. #54 – You have a time-based OCD.
19. #55 – You're immortal.
20. #58 – Everything's happening in slow motion.
21. #59– You find a pocket watch. Engraved on the back reads "Now it's your turn".
22. #62 – The ability to speak to and understand animals.
23. #63 – You are a crossbreed between a human and a mystical creature.
24. #65 – A dinosaur egg just hatched at your local museum.
25. #67 – Down the rabbit hole we go.
26. #70 – You've discovered a new species.

27. #71 – You've just gotten a dog – only, it's not a dog.
28. #74 – An animal that can speak English.
29. #75 – You've been transformed into an animal.
30. #81 – An animal has come back from extinction.
31. #82 – You've found a creature frozen in the tundra of Antarctica.
32. #83 – You've found a creature lurking in the depths of the ocean.
33. #85 – A world run by animals.
34. #86 – All animals have begun to mysteriously die off.
35. #92 – The AI in your phone is trying to warn you.
36. #93 – Your car has taken over and is taking you somewhere.
37. #94 – You've fallen in love with an AI.
38. #95 – The world has been taken over by robots.
39. #97 – You've ripped out your tracker chip. Now what?
40. #98 – An injector is pumping poison into the Earth.
41. #99 – You wake up in the hospital with a mechanical arm.
42. #100 – Your brain has been downloaded into a robotic body.
43. #101 – Someone is wiping all your evidence from your hard drives.
44. #102 – Your record player is repeating very specific phrases.
45. #104 – All technology has been outlawed.
46. #106 – The government is hiding technology lightyears beyond what the masses have access to.
47. #107 – Humans have created a serum for immortality.
48. #108 – You're on a team trying to stop an asteroid from colliding with Earth.
49. #109 – While showering, you find an "on/off" tattoo on your body.
50. #110 – You're working on something that could win your side the war.
51. #112 – You volunteer to test the newest technological breakthrough – but something goes wrong.
52. #113 – A robot comes to your home and shows you a projection of someone asking for help.
53. #114 – You find a foreign piece of technology. It almost seems … alien.
54. #116 – You toss something in a pile at the junk yard and something turns on.
55. #119 – "We didn't have this back in my day."
56. #121 – People's memories are being erased.

57. #122 – Area 51 is nothing like you expected.
58. #127 – You're on an alien planet – with no way to get back home.
59. #137 – Were you just … teleported?
60. #142 – "Where the hell do you think you're going?"
61. #153 – You've discovered the cure for cancer – inside a government vault.
62. #154 – Something's growing in your boss' lab.
63. #155 – Scientists have figured out how to bring the dead back to life.
64. #156 – A new metal has been discovered – and it's being used in … interesting ways.
65. #157 – There is now a weekly pill you can take to keep you from aging.
66. #159 – Some kids in your neighbor's garage may or may not have just successfully created a teleportation machine.
67. #161 – The new scientist in your department is a little sketchy …
68. #162 – The world's greatest scientists have banded together to take over the world.
69. #164 – Scientific law as we know it is falling apart.
70. #165 – Aliens have agreed to share their scientific knowledge with us.
71. #167 – Science has been set back by 50 years.
72. #168 – The sun is going to explode millions of years ahead of schedule.
73. #169 – Scientists have figured out how to bring extinct animals back to life by using their remains to create clones.
74. #171 – The moon is starting to leave Earth's orbit.
75. #173 – What would Earth be like one thousand years into the future?
76. #176 – "We've done it! We've found the cure!"
77. #177 – A device that allows people to control others as if they were a videogame character.
78. #180 – "This defies everything we know of space and time."
79. #181 – A scientist has just discovered the secret to immortality but is hesitant to reveal it to the world.
80. #182 – Your spaceship has blown an engine on your way to your destination.
81. #190 – Regret.

82. #193 – Curiosity.
83. #198 – Hope.
84. #206 – Selfish.
85. #210 – Defiant.
86. #212 – Disappointed.
87. #216 – You've got food poisoning.
88. #222 – "I'm so sick of this packaged dehydrated crap."
89. #224 – It's fondue night!
90. #229 – You've burnt it – again.
91. #233 – You've entered an eating contest.
92. #237 – Your child is having an allergic reaction.
93. #243 – You're so full you could pop.
94. #245 – You've just discovered your great grandfather was a necromancer.
95. #256 – "Hurry up and cast the spell!"
96. #258 – You're on the verge of creating a new magic system.
97. #259 – A camera that creates 2D clones.
98. #270 – Each time a spell is cast, the planet grows closer to death.
99. #278 – You spot a mermaid while out fishing.
100. #281 – A device that allows you to read people's minds.
101. #282 – People are starting to age backwards.
102. #286 – Something is lurking in the shadows.
103. #287 – A cure is being researched for vampirism.
104. #291 – Humans are being harvested to produce blood for vampires.
105. #294 – Humans have become nocturnal.
106. #299 – The full moon's light is acidic.
107. #300 – A cure is being researched for zombies.
108. #304 – A cure is being researched for werewolves.
109. #311 – World domination.
110. #313 – A villain has placed several bombs throughout your city.
111. #320 – "Must you ruin everything?"
112. #325 – "I'm going to burn this world to the ground."
113. #327 – A villain's costume.
114. #332 – Notorious.
115. #334 – A villain driven by logic.
116. #338 – Extension.
117. #339 – Laptop.
118. #342 – Stationary.

119. #348 – Fire.
120. #350 – Plant.
121. #355 – Bubble.
122. #360 – Number.
123. #364 – Fly.

Romance (R)

1. #4 – You've just won a date with your favorite celebrity. They're picking you up tonight at 7PM.
2. #5 – "Where were you last night?"
3. #6 – You can't keep your eyes off the new intern.
4. #12 – You receive a letter from your ex-fiancé.
5. #13 – Someone picks you up hitchhiking.
6. #18 – You're about to meet an author who has changed your life.
7. #19 – You find someone sitting on your porch.
8. #22 – Your best friend's lover has just confessed their love for you.
9. #36 – You've got a blind date at 8PM.
10. #40 – "When?"
11. #52 – If you could change one thing from your past, what would it be?
12. #55 – You're immortal.
13. #57 – The dragons soar through the skies every night at dusk.
14. #59– You find a pocket watch. Engraved on the back reads "Now it's your turn".
15. #68 – "You dog, you."
16. #76 – You've found out your lover is a shapeshifter.
17. #94 – You've fallen in love with an AI.
18. #96 – The latest phone has the craziest new feature.
19. #99 – You wake up in the hospital with a mechanical arm.
20. #100 – Your brain has been downloaded into a robotic body.
21. #104 – All technology has been outlawed.
22. #107 – Humans have created a serum for immortality.
23. #111 – Your computer screen goes black. A message appears.
24. #115 – "Technology is great when it decides to work."
25. #122 – Area 51 is nothing like you expected.
26. #125 – You've just won a vacation to your favorite place.
27. #131 – A blind date is meeting you at a café in 20 minutes.

28. #133 – Road trip
29. #139 – "Where you go, I go."
30. #143 – You've just woken up in the hospital with no memory of how you got there.
31. #146 – You are undeniably, undoubtably, indescribably – lost.
32. #158 – The internet is now at your fingertips – literally.
33. #166 – "Good god … what have you done?!"
34. #170 – "If only we had the money to fund our research …"
35. #172 – "There appears to be a chemical reaction happening …"
36. #174 – What would your field of research be if you were a scientist?
37. #177 – A device that allows people to control others as if they were a videogame character.
38. #179 – Never fall in love with your experiments.
39. #184 – Rage.
40. #186 – Love.
41. #191 – Joy.
42. #194 – Relaxed.
43. #197 – Frustration.
44. #199 – Lust.
45. #201 – Nostalgia.
46. #205 – Cautious.
47. #207 – Flirtatious.
48. #210 – Defiant.
49. #213 – Heartbroken.
50. #214 – Satisfied.
51. #215 – Breakfast.
52. #219 – You have an apprenticeship with your favorite chef.
53. #221 – Dessert.
54. #223 – Your partner has surprised you with your favorite meal.
55. #227 – Someone has poisoned the buffet at a presidential speech.
56. #229 – You've burnt it – again.
57. #231 – Chocolate-covered strawberries.
58. #234 – "I said tomatoes, not potatoes!"
59. #236 – Something is burning …
60. #241 – Something smells good!
61. #242 – You and your partner are out on a picnic.
62. #246 – When dusting off an old bottle in the attic, a genie emerges.
63. #248 – Your fiancé has been cursed.

64. #249 – You are half human, half witch/wizard.
65. #253 – This spell enables you to inhabit someone's body for a day.
66. #257 – You've been turned into a phoenix.
67. #260 – Fortune cookies actually tell fortunes.
68. #265 – "Are you *trying* to hex me? Because, rude."
69. #271 – The ability to manipulate the elements.
70. #272 – "Do you think we could get them to write that scroll for us?"
71. #277 – You spot someone using supernatural abilities – and they want you to keep quiet about it.
72. #280 – Vampires.
73. #282 – People are starting to age backwards.
74. #285 – A new species of humans has started to emerge.
75. #287 – A cure is being researched for vampirism.
76. #298 – The ability to erase memories.
77. #301 – "Have you come for my soul?"
78. #302 – Your guardian angel hates you.
79. #308 – Infamous.
80. #314 – Your best friend has decided to join the bad guys.
81. #320 – "Must you ruin everything?"
82. #323 – "I'd always wanted to be a hero … Funny how the world works."
83. #324 – You've fallen for the villain.
84. #329 – "You're letting me go? Aren't you the bad guy?"
85. #333 – "The hero life's never done anything for me."
86. #335 – A villain driven by emotion.
87. #340 – Fleece.
88. #341 – DVD.
89. #346 – Chair.
90. #348 – Fire.
91. #352 – Plush.
92. #353 – Decline.
93. #356 – Box.
94. #359 – Switch.
95. #360 – Number.

Mystery (M)

1. #1 – You've discovered a long lost relative.
2. #5 – "Where were you last night?"
3. #6 – You can't keep your eyes off the new intern.
4. #7 – You've been given a treasure map by a homeless man.
5. #8 – You've just found out that your best friend is an alien.
6. #9 – You've been hired as a private investigator.
7. #12 – You receive a letter from your ex-fiance.
8. #13 – Someone picks you up hitchhiking.
9. #19 – You find someone sitting on your porch.
10. #20 – Someone's child is lost in the park.
11. #22 – Your best friend's lover has just confessed their love for you.
12. #25 – A killer is on the loose in your town.
13. #29 – You're one of the last humans to survive.
14. #33 – There's a ticking time-bomb. Red wire, or blue?
15. #34 – You wake up 100 years into the future.
16. #35 – You wake up 100 years into the past.
17. #36 – You've got a blind date at 8PM.
18. #40 – "When?"
19. #45 – All of the clocks in your home have stopped.
20. #49 – "Get here by noon, or she dies."
21. #51 – If you had the ability to see your future, would you?
22. #54 – You have a time-based OCD.
23. #58 – Everything's happening in slow motion.
24. #68 – "You dog, you."
25. #73 – Search hounds are hunting you down.
26. #76 – You've found out your lover is a shapeshifter.
27. #79 – Animals are escaping from your local zoo.
28. #82 – You've found a creature frozen in the tundra of Antarctica.
29. #84 – There's something aboard your ship – and it's hungry.
30. #86 – All animals have begun to mysteriously die off.
31. #88 – The oceans are being poisoned.
32. #90 – You do some bird calls in the woods - and something else answers.
33. #91 – You find a wild horse nursing a unicorn.
34. #92 – The AI in your phone is trying to warn you.
35. #98 – An injector is pumping poison into the Earth.

36. #101 – Someone is wiping all your evidence from your hard drives.
37. #102 – Your record player is repeating very specific phrases.
38. #106 – The government is hiding technology lightyears beyond what the masses have access to.
39. #108 – You're on a team trying to stop an asteroid from colliding with Earth.
40. #109 – While showering, you find an "on/off" tattoo on your body.
41. #111 – Your computer screen goes black. A message appears.
42. #113 – A robot comes to your home and shows you a projection of someone asking for help.
43. #114 – You find a foreign piece of technology. It almost seems … alien.
44. #116 – You toss something in a pile at the junk yard and something turns on.
45. #118 – Planned obsoletion.
46. #120 – This new tech is going to change the world.
47. #121 – People's memories are being erased.
48. #123 – You've just broken out of your containment module.
49. #124 – "How the hell did I end up here?"
50. #126 – "… Where are we?"
51. #128 – "How can they be in two places at once?"
52. #129 – Next stop – the White House.
53. #131 – A blind date is meeting you at a café in 20 minutes.
54. #132 – You're stranded on a deserted island.
55. #135 – "Where did you last see them?"
56. #141 – "Where are you taking me?"
57. #143 – You've just woken up in the hospital with no memory of how you got there.
58. #145 – "Meet me in the lobby in 10 minutes."
59. #146 – You are undeniably, undoubtably, indescribably – lost.
60. #152 – "Ugh, I don't want to go."
61. #153 – You've discovered the cure for cancer – inside a government vault.
62. #156 – A new metal has been discovered – and it's being used in … interesting ways.
63. #160 – "This breakthrough could save mankind."
64. #161 – The new scientist in your department is a little sketchy …
65. #164 – Scientific law as we know it is falling apart.

66. #166 – "Good god … what have you done?!"
67. #167 – Science has been set back by 50 years.
68. #168 – The sun is going to explode millions of years ahead of schedule.
69. #171 – The moon is starting to leave Earth's orbit.
70. #173 – What would Earth be like one thousand years into the future?
71. #176 – "We've done it! We've found the cure!"
72. #179 – Never fall in love with your experiments.
73. #181 – A scientist has just discovered the secret to immortality but is hesitant to reveal it to the world.
74. #185 – Uncertainty.
75. #188 – Sorrow.
76. #189 – Relief.
77. #192 – Denial.
78. #195 – Stressed.
79. #197 – Frustration.
80. #204 – Worry.
81. #208 – Giddy.
82. #211 – Submissive.
83. #213 – Heartbroken.
84. #216 – You've got food poisoning.
85. #220 – You start as a waitress tomorrow night.
86. #225 – A la mode.
87. #227 – Someone has poisoned the buffet at a presidential speech.
88. #230 – You're learning a new recipe.
89. #232 – You find a child going through your trash for food.
90. #235 – People start to go missing right around the time a new restaurant opens.
91. #238 – Rats are nibbling away at a dead body you've come across in an alley.
92. #241 – Something smells good!
93. #247 – You cast a spell with one intention – but something completely different happens.
94. #252 – "If we cast the spell together, we can take it down!"
95. #254 – What happens when you accidently cast a curse?
96. #257 – You've been turned into a phoenix.
97. #263 – Modern witch/wizard.
98. #265 – "Are you trying to hex me? Because, rude."

99. #267 – You wear magic restraints to keep your power under control.
100. #268 – "The book of forbidden spells … it's gone missing."
101. #270 – Each time a spell is cast, the planet grows closer to death.
102. #272 – "Do you think we could get them to write that scroll for us?"
103. #274 – All magic has been outlawed.
104. #276 – A werewolf has been reported lurking just outside your town.
105. #281 – A device that allows you to read people's minds.
106. #282 – People are starting to age backwards.
107. #283 – A nuclear explosion has started to give people strange abilities.
108. #289 – Their mission is to assassinate the king.
109. #293 – Sirens are created when someone dies violently at sea.
110. #295 – The afterlife has a receptionist.
111. #303 – "The world's changed. It's best if you do, too."
112. #304 – A cure is being researched for werewolves.
113. #307 – Evil henchmen.
114. #310 – You've taken an internship as an evil sidekick.
115. #312 – "You'll never stop me!"
116. #313 – A villain has placed several bombs throughout your city.
117. #318 – Severed limbs are showing up on people's doorsteps.
118. #322 – Someone forced to be evil.
119. #326 – A hero undercover as a villain.
120. #328 – An adult villain can't bring themselves to fight an underaged hero.
121. #331 – Someone thought to be a villain is actually the hero.
122. #333 – "The hero life's never done anything for me."
123. #336 – The villain realizes they're wrong.
124. #339 – Laptop.
125. #341 – DVD.
126. #344 – Tunnel.
127. #347 – Deer.
128. #351 – Frame.
129. #355 – Bubble.
130. #359 – Switch.
131. #365 – Board.

Horror (H)

1. #3 – Someone has just broken into your home with malicious intent.
2. #4 – You've just won a date with your favorite celebrity. They're picking you up tonight at 7PM.
3. #8 – You've just found out that your best friend is an alien.
4. #10 – You are given the opportunity to meet the person that has given you one of their kidneys.
5. #11 – You are watching your loved one turn into a zombie.
6. #13 – Someone picks you up hitchhiking.
7. #17 -There's a ghost living in your attic.
8. #20 – Someone's child is lost in the park.
9. #23 – You're having a family reunion.
10. #24 – A loved one is brought back to life – for a price.
11. #25 – A killer is on the loose in your town.
12. #26 – You're at the wrong place at the wrong time.
13. #28 – You're being hunted down.
14. #32 – You're running out of time.
15. #39 – "You've got ten seconds."
16. #41 – It's 2AM and you can't sleep.
17. #44 – You've got one minute to sever your arm, or you'll die.
18. #61 – Cats with opposable thumbs.
19. #64 – Flying monkeys!
20. #65 – A dinosaur egg just hatched at your local museum.
21. #69 – "Yeah, when pigs fly."
22. #70 – You've discovered a new species.
23. #71 – You've just gotten a dog – only, it's not a dog.
24. #80 – You are face to face with a wary wildcat.
25. #81 – An animal has come back from extinction.
26. #83 – You've found a creature lurking in the depths of the ocean.
27. #84 – There's something aboard your ship – and it's hungry.
28. #87 – A fishing trip gone wrong.
29. #90 – You do some bird calls in the woods - and something else answers.
30. #92 – The AI in your phone is trying to warn you.
31. #95 – The world has been taken over by robots.
32. #102 – Your record player is repeating very specific phrases.
33. #103 – You're in a toy store when all of the remote-controlled cars start heading towards you.

34. #112 – You volunteer to test the newest technological breakthrough – but something goes wrong.
35. #121 – People's memories are being erased.
36. #125 – You've just won a vacation to your favorite place.
37. #126 – "… Where are we?"
38. #130 – You need to find your way out of a locked room – and fast.
39. #132 – You're stranded on a deserted island.
40. #134 – This place feels totally different at night.
41. #135 – "Where did you last see them?"
42. #138 – You're at the wrong place at the wrong time.
43. #141 – "Where are you taking me?"
44. #149 – "I just want to go home."
45. #154 – Something's growing in your boss' lab.
46. #155 – Scientists have figured out how to bring the dead back to life.
47. #160 – "This breakthrough could save mankind."
48. #161 – The new scientist in your department is a little sketchy …
49. #166 – "Good god … what have you done?!"
50. #168 – The sun is going to explode millions of years ahead of schedule.
51. #171 – The moon is starting to leave Earth's orbit.
52. #175 – Climate change has set the world in crisis.
53. #179 – Never fall in love with your experiments.
54. #181 – A scientist has just discovered the secret to immortality but is hesitant to reveal it to the world.
55. #187 – Desperation.
56. #190 – Regret.
57. #192 – Denial.
58. #195 – Stressed.
59. #203 – Depression.
60. #208 – Giddy.
61. #213 – Heartbroken.
62. #217 – "This is delicious!"
63. #225 – A la mode.
64. #226 – "Three second rule."
65. #230 – You're learning a new recipe.
66. #233 – You've entered an eating contest.
67. #235 – People start to go missing right around the time a new restaurant opens.

68. #237 – Your child is having an allergic reaction.
69. #238 – Rats are nibbling away at a dead body you've come across in an alley.
70. #240 – Dinner.
71. #244 – You're starving.
72. #247 – You cast a spell with one intention – but something completely different happens.
73. #248 – Your fiancé has been cursed.
74. #253 – This spell enables you to inhabit someone's body for a day.
75. #254 – What happens when you accidently cast a curse?
76. #260 – Fortune cookies actually tell fortunes.
77. #261 – You are a master of the dark arts.
78. #262 – You cast the wrong spell and all hell breaks loose – literally.
79. #265 – "Are you trying to hex me? Because, rude."
80. #269 – The ability to control shadows.
81. #270 – Each time a spell is cast, the planet grows closer to death.
82. #273 – You've summoned the wrong mystical creature.
83. #276 – A werewolf has been reported lurking just outside your town.
84. #279 – After a hard hit to the head, you're starting to see supernatural creatures everywhere you look.
85. #284 – The zombie apocalypse has begun.
86. #286 – Something is lurking in the shadows.
87. #290 – Mermaids are learning to live on land.
88. #291 – Humans are being harvested to produce blood for vampires.
89. #292 – Demons are walking among us.
90. #293 – Sirens are created when someone dies violently at sea.
91. #296 – Monsters are flooding in from the sky.
92. #297 – A woman has adopted Lucifer's child.
93. #299 – The full moon's light is acidic.
94. #300 – A cure is being researched for zombies.
95. #305 – You can have any wish granted – for a price.
96. #307 – Evil henchmen.
97. #309 – Someone has kidnapped you and is holding you hostage.
98. #313 – A villain has placed several bombs throughout your city.
99. #315 – A villain posing as a damsel in distress.
100. #316 – Rotten to the core.

101. #318 – Severed limbs are showing up on people's doorsteps.
102. #325 – "I'm going to burn this world to the ground."
103. #329 – "You're letting me go? Aren't you the bad guy?"
104. #332 – Notorious.
105. #334 – A villain driven by logic.
106. #337 – Crossbow.
107. #343 – Void.
108. #344 – Tunnel.
109. #350 – Plant.
110. #353 – Decline.
111. #356 – Box.
112. #358 – Curtain.
113. #361 – Stage.
114. #365 – Board.

Dystopian (D)

1. #11 – You are watching your loved one turn into a zombie.
2. #15 – People are cheering your name.
3. #21 – "What have you done?"
4. #29 – You're one of the last humans to survive.
5. #31 – You regret your decision.
6. #46 – It starts at midnight. Hope you're ready.
7. #47 – "What a time to be alive."
8. #49 – "Get here by noon, or she dies."
9. #56 – "There's no time! Go!"
10. #61 – Cats with opposable thumbs.
11. #66 – You're a dragon tamer.
12. #73 – Search hounds are hunting you down.
13. #85 – A world run by animals.
14. #86 – All animals have begun to mysteriously die off.
15. #95 – The world has been taken over by robots.
16. #96 – The latest phone has the craziest new feature.
17. #97 – You've ripped out your tracker chip. Now what?
18. #100 – Your brain has been downloaded into a robotic body.
19. #104 – All technology has been outlawed.
20. #105 – All technology has been strictly reserved for the upper-class.

21. #106 – The government is hiding technology lightyears beyond what the masses have access to.
22. #111 – Your computer screen goes black. A message appears.
23. #116 – You toss something in a pile at the junk yard and something turns on.
24. #118 – Planned obsoletion.
25. #120 – This new tech is going to change the world.
26. #123 – You've just broken out of your containment module.
27. #129 – Next stop – the White House.
28. #136 – Go to your happy place. They won't find you there.
29. #138 – You're at the wrong place at the wrong time.
30. #144 – "This isn't the time or the place for that."
31. #149 – "I just want to go home."
32. #150 – You've got the map – now you just need someone who can read it.
33. #153 – You've discovered the cure for cancer – inside a government vault.
34. #156 – A new metal has been discovered – and it's being used in … interesting ways.
35. #157 – There is now a weekly pill you can take to keep you from aging.
36. #160 – "This breakthrough could save mankind."
37. #164 – Scientific law as we know it is falling apart.
38. #167 – Science has been set back by 50 years.
39. #170 – "If only we had the money to fund our research …"
40. #173 – What would Earth be like one thousand years into the future?
41. #175 – Climate change has set the world in crisis.
42. #178 – A device that lets you slow or quick your eyes frame rate.
43. #185 – Uncertainty.
44. #187 – Desperation.
45. #192 – Denial.
46. #196 – Fatigue.
47. #200 – Hatred.
48. #203 – Depression.
49. #206 – Selfish.
50. #208 – Giddy.
51. #209 – Determined.
52. #218 – You've just been accepted into the culinary school of your dreams.

53. #221 – Dessert.
54. #222 – "I'm so sick of this packaged dehydrated crap."
55. #226 – "Three second rule."
56. #233 – You've entered an eating contest.
57. #238 – Rats are nibbling away at a dead body you've come across in an alley.
58. #244 – You're starving.
59. #252 – "If we cast the spell together, we can take it down!"
60. #267 – You wear magic restraints to keep your power under control.
61. #273 – You've summoned the wrong mystical creature.
62. #274 – All magic has been outlawed.
63. #277 – You spot someone using supernatural abilities – and they want you to keep quiet about it.
64. #280 – Vampires.
65. #283 – A nuclear explosion has started to give people strange abilities.
66. #284 – The zombie apocalypse has begun.
67. #288 – Each zodiac sign is granted a set range of abilities.
68. #292 – Demons are walking among us.
69. #296 – Monsters are flooding in from the sky.
70. #303 – "The world's changed. It's best if you do, too."
71. #306 – "Impossible!"
72. #311 – World domination.
73. #312 – "You'll never stop me!"
74. #315 – A villain posing as a damsel in distress.
75. #317 – A retired villain now serving as an advisor to heroes.
76. #322 – Someone forced to be evil.
77. #326 – A hero undercover as a villain.
78. #330 – "Who's ready to get in a little trouble?"
79. #336 – The villain realizes they're wrong.
80. #340 – Fleece.
81. #346 – Chair.
82. #349 – Steps.
83. #355 – Bubble.
84. #359 – Switch.
85. #362 – Show.
86. #363 – Sun.

Action & Adventure (AA)

1. #2 – You run into yourself in a dream, but something isn't right – they're trying their hardest to stay away from you.
2. #3 – Someone has just broken into your home with malicious intent.
3. #7 – You've been given a treasure map by a homeless man.
4. #15 – People are cheering your name.
5. #16 – You're a pirate preparing to set sail.
6. #23 – You're having a family reunion.
7. #25 – A killer is on the loose in your town.
8. #26 – You're at the wrong place at the wrong time.
9. #28 – You're being hunted down.
10. #30 – "You'll pay for this!"
11. #32 – You're running out of time.
12. #33 – There's a ticking time-bomb. Red wire, or blue?
13. #34 – You wake up 100 years into the future.
14. #35 – You wake up 100 years into the past.
15. #37 – "Any second now."
16. #38 – "We don't have time for this!"
17. #39 – "You've got ten seconds."
18. #42 – The only way to save the future, is to destroy the past.
19. #43 – You're tired of waiting. It's time to take action.
20. #44 – You've got one minute to sever your arm, or you'll die.
21. #46 – It starts at midnight. Hope you're ready.
22. #48 – Your spell will only last for two minutes.
23. #56 – "There's no time! Go!"
24. #59– You find a pocket watch. Engraved on the back reads "Now it's your turn".
25. #60 – You're face to face with Father Time.
26. #65 – A dinosaur egg just hatched at your local museum.
27. #66 – You're a dragon tamer.
28. #67 – Down the rabbit hole we go.
29. #72 – There's something growling out there in the darkness.
30. #73 – Search hounds are hunting you down.
31. #78 – "Get that thing out of here!"
32. #79 – Animals are escaping from your local zoo.
33. #80 – You are face to face with a wary wildcat.
34. #82 – You've found a creature frozen in the tundra of Antarctica.
35. #83 – You've found a creature lurking in the depths of the ocean.

36. #87 – A fishing trip gone wrong.
37. #88 – The oceans are being poisoned.
38. #90 – You do some bird calls in the woods - and something else answers.
39. #93 – Your car has taken over and is taking you somewhere.
40. #97 – You've ripped out your tracker chip. Now what?
41. #99 – You wake up in the hospital with a mechanical arm.
42. #101 – Someone is wiping all your evidence from your hard drives.
43. #103 – You're in a toy store when all of the remote-controlled cars start heading towards you.
44. #105 – All technology has been strictly reserved for the upper-class.
45. #108 – You're on a team trying to stop an asteroid from colliding with Earth.
46. #109 – While showering, you find an "on/off" tattoo on your body.
47. #110 – You're working on something that could win your side the war.
48. #113 – A robot comes to your home and shows you a projection of someone asking for help.
49. #117 – "Dammit! Why won't this stupid thing work?!"
50. #123 – You've just broken out of your containment module.
51. #124 – "How the hell did I end up here?"
52. #128 – "How can they be in two places at once?"
53. #130 – You need to find your way out of a locked room – and fast.
54. #132 – You're stranded on a deserted island.
55. #137 – Were you just … teleported?
56. #139 – "Where you go, I go."
57. #140 – Someone offers to take you to a magical place. Will you go?
58. #142 – "Where the hell do you think you're going?"
59. #145 – "Meet me in the lobby in 10 minutes."
60. #149 – "I just want to go home."
61. #150 – You've got the map – now you just need someone who can read it.
62. #151 – You never thought you'd be on the other side of a prison cell.
63. #158 – The internet is now at your fingertips – literally.

393

64. #162 – The world's greatest scientists have banded together to take over the world.
65. #169 – Scientists have figured out how to bring extinct animals back to life by using their remains to create clones.
66. #178 – A device that lets you slow or quick your eyes frame rate.
67. #180 – "This defies everything we know of space and time."
68. #182 – Your spaceship has blown an engine on your way to your destination.
69. #184 – Rage.
70. #188 – Sorrow.
71. #190 – Regret.
72. #201 – Nostalgia.
73. #202 – Guilt.
74. #205 – Cautious.
75. #209 – Determined.
76. #212 – Disappointed.
77. #218 – You've just been accepted into the culinary school of your dreams.
78. #220 – You start as a waitress tomorrow night.
79. #222 – "I'm so sick of this packaged dehydrated crap."
80. #227 – Someone has poisoned the buffet at a presidential speech.
81. #234 – "I said tomatoes, not potatoes!"
82. #236 – Something is burning …
83. #239 – You're on the search for a rare fruit in the amazon.
84. #244 – You're starving.
85. #251 – A spell that was once keeping an evil overlord imprisoned has just been broken.
86. #252 – "If we cast the spell together, we can take it down!"
87. #256 – "Hurry up and cast the spell!"
88. #261 – You are a master of the dark arts.
89. #263 – Modern witch/wizard.
90. #264 – Teacher by day, witch hunter by night.
91. #268 – "The book of forbidden spells … it's gone missing."
92. #273 – You've summoned the wrong mystical creature.
93. #274 – All magic has been outlawed.
94. #278 – You spot a mermaid while out fishing.
95. #283 – A nuclear explosion has started to give people strange abilities.
96. #289 – Their mission is to assassinate the king.
97. #293 – Sirens are created when someone dies violently at sea.

98. #296 – Monsters are flooding in from the sky.
99. #303 – "The world's changed. It's best if you do, too."
100. #304 – A cure is being researched for werewolves.
101. #306 – "Impossible!"
102. #309 – Someone has kidnapped you and is holding you hostage.
103. #312 – "You'll never stop me!"
104. #315 – A villain posing as a damsel in distress.
105. #317 – A retired villain now serving as an advisor to heroes.
106. #319 – Evil lair.
107. #324 – You've fallen for the villain.
108. #326 – A hero undercover as a villain.
109. #328 – An adult villain can't bring themselves to fight an underaged hero.
110. #331 – Someone thought to be a villain is actually the hero.
111. #336 – The villain realizes they're wrong.
112. #337 – Crossbow.
113. #342 – Stationary.
114. #344 – Tunnel.
115. #347 – Deer.
116. #350 – Plant.
117. #353 – Decline.
118. #354 – Gold.
119. #357 – Grind.
120. #361 – Stage.
121. #363 – Sun.
122. #364 – Fly.

Paranormal (P)

1. #10 – You are given the opportunity to meet the person that has given you one of their kidneys.
2. #11 – You are watching your loved one turn into a zombie.
3. #14 – "Don't you dare."
4. #17 -There's a ghost living in your attic.
5. #21 – "What have you done?"
6. #24 – A loved one is brought back to life – for a price.
7. #41 – It's 2AM and you can't sleep.
8. #45 – All of the clocks in your home have stopped.
9. #67 – Down the rabbit hole we go.

10. #78 – "Get that thing out of here!"
11. #89 – The spirit of a lost pet lingers around your house.
12. #115 – "Technology is great when it decides to work."
13. #117 – "Dammit! Why won't this stupid thing work?!"
14. #130 – You need to find your way out of a locked room – and fast.
15. #134 – This place feels totally different at night.
16. #139 – "Where you go, I go."
17. #143 – You've just woken up in the hospital with no memory of how you got there.
18. #152 – "Ugh, I don't want to go."
19. #155 – Scientists have figured out how to bring the dead back to life.
20. #163 – Your scientific experiment is about to go horribly, horribly wrong.
21. #172 – "There appears to be a chemical reaction happening …"
22. #183 – "Tell Dr. Garner I'll be with him in a moment."
23. #185 – Uncertainty.
24. #187 – Desperation.
25. #196 – Fatigue.
26. #200 – Hatred.
27. #202 – Guilt.
28. #205 – Cautious.
29. #212 – Disappointed.
30. #219 – You have an apprenticeship with your favorite chef.
31. #224 – It's fondue night!
32. #228 – Lunch.
33. #231 – Chocolate-covered strawberries.
34. #235 – People start to go missing right around the time a new restaurant opens.
35. #240 – Dinner.
36. #247 – You cast a spell with one intention – but something completely different happens.
37. #251 – A spell that was once keeping an evil overlord imprisoned has just been broken.
38. #255 – You're called on in the audience by a magician on stage.
39. #259 – A camera that creates 2D clones.
40. #266 – A conversation with your reflection.
41. #279 – After a hard hit to the head, you're starting to see supernatural creatures everywhere you loo

42. #285 – A new species of humans has started to emerge.
43. #294 – Humans have become nocturnal.
44. #295 – The afterlife has a receptionist.
45. #301 – "Have you come for my soul?"
46. #308 – Infamous.
47. #316 – Rotten to the core.
48. #318 – Severed limbs are showing up on people's doorsteps.
49. #322 – Someone forced to be evil.
50. #325 – "I'm going to burn this world to the ground."
51. #329 – "You're letting me go? Aren't you the bad guy?"
52. #335 – A villain driven by emotion.
53. #339 – Laptop.
54. #342 – Stationary.
55. #343 – Void.
56. #346 – Chair.
57. #352 – Plush.
58. #357 – Grind.
59. #358 – Curtain.
60. #364 – Fly.

Slice of Life (SL)

1. #1 – You've discovered a long lost relative.
2. #3 – Someone has just broken into your home with malicious intent.
3. #4 – You've just won a date with your favorite celebrity. They're picking you up tonight at 7PM.
4. #5 – "Where were you last night?"
5. #6 – You can't keep your eyes off the new intern.
6. #10 – You are given the opportunity to meet the person that has given you one of their kidneys.
7. #12 – You receive a letter from your ex-fiance.
8. #14 – "Don't you dare."
9. #15 – People are cheering your name.
10. #18 – You're about to meet an author who has changed your life.
11. #19 – You find someone sitting on your porch.
12. #20 – Someone's child is lost in the park.
13. #21 – "What have you done?"

14. #22 – Your best friend's lover has just confessed their love for you.
15. #23 – You're having a family reunion.
16. #26 – You're at the wrong place at the wrong time.
17. #30 – "You'll pay for this!"
18. #31 – You regret your decision.
19. #32 – You're running out of time.
20. #36 – You've got a blind date at 8PM.
21. #37 – "Any second now."
22. #38 – "We don't have time for this!"
23. #39 – "You've got ten seconds."
24. #40 – "When?"
25. #41 – It's 2AM and you can't sleep.
26. #43 – You're tired of waiting. It's time to take action.
27. #47 – "What a time to be alive."
28. #49 – "Get here by noon, or she dies."
29. #50 – "Good timing."
30. #52 – If you could change one thing from your past, what would it be?
31. #54 – You have a time-based OCD.
32. #57 – The dragons soar through the skies every night at dusk.
33. #64 – Flying monkeys!
34. #68 – "You dog, you."
35. #69 – "Yeah, when pigs fly."
36. #70 – You've discovered a new species.
37. #72 – There's something growling out there in the darkness.
38. #75 – You've been transformed into an animal.
39. #79 – Animals are escaping from your local zoo.
40. #80 – You are face to face with a wary wildcat.
41. #85 – A world run by animals.
42. #87 – A fishing trip gone wrong.
43. #88 – The oceans are being poisoned.
44. #89 – The spirit of a lost pet lingers around your house.
45. #94 – You've fallen in love with an AI.
46. #96 – The latest phone has the craziest new feature.
47. #105 – All technology has been strictly reserved for the upper-class.
48. #112 – You volunteer to test the newest technological breakthrough – but something goes wrong.
49. #118 – Planned obsoletion.

50. #120 – This new tech is going to change the world.
51. #124 – "How the hell did I end up here?"
52. #125 – You've just won a vacation to your favorite place.
53. #129 – Next stop – the White House.
54. #131 – A blind date is meeting you at a café in 20 minutes.
55. #133 – Road trip!
56. #135 – "Where did you last see them?"
57. #141 – "Where are you taking me?"
58. #142 – "Where the hell do you think you're going?"
59. #144 – "This isn't the time or the place for that."
60. #146 – You are undeniably, undoubtably, indescribably – lost.
61. #147 – So this is what heaven look like.
62. #148 – So this is what hell looks like.
63. #151 – You never thought you'd be on the other side of a prison cell.
64. #152 – "Ugh, I don't want to go."
65. #157 – There is now a weekly pill you can take to keep you from aging.
66. #159 – Some kids in your neighbor's garage may or may not have just successfully created a teleportation machine.
67. #169 – Scientists have figured out how to bring extinct animals back to life by using their remains to create clones.
68. #170 – "If only we had the money to fund our research …"
69. #174 – What would your field of research be if you were a scientist?
70. #175 – Climate change has set the world in crisis.
71. #177 – A device that allows people to control others as if they were a videogame character.
72. #182 – Your spaceship has blown an engine on your way to your destination.
73. #183 – "Tell Dr. Garner I'll be with him in a moment."
74. #186 – Love.
75. #189 – Relief.
76. #191 – Joy.
77. #193 – Curiosity.
78. #194 – Relaxed.
79. #195 – Stressed.
80. #198 – Hope.
81. #200 – Hatred.
82. #202 – Guilt.

83. #203 – Depression.
84. #206 – Selfish.
85. #207 – Flirtatious.
86. #210 – Defiant.
87. #211 – Submissive.
88. #214 – Satisfied.
89. #215 – Breakfast.
90. #216 – You've got food poisoning.
91. #218 – You've just been accepted into the culinary school of your dreams.
92. #221 – Dessert.
93. #223 – Your partner has surprised you with your favorite meal.
94. #226 – "Three second rule."
95. #228 – Lunch.
96. #230 – You're learning a new recipe.
97. #232 – You find a child going through your trash for food.
98. #234 – "I said tomatoes, not potatoes!"
99. #237 – Your child is having an allergic reaction.
100. #240 – Dinner.
101. #242 – You and your partner are out on a picnic.
102. #243 – You're so full you could pop.
103. #246 – When dusting off an old bottle in the attic, a genie emerges.
104. #249 – You are half human, half witch/wizard.
105. #250 – You're trying to learn some magic tricks.
106. #255 – You're called on in the audience by a magician on stage.
107. #260 – Fortune cookies actually tell fortunes.
108. #263 – Modern witch/wizard.
109. #266 – A conversation with your reflection.
110. #275 – You've been chosen to be your magic art school's successor.
111. #277 – You spot someone using supernatural abilities – and they want you to keep quiet about it.
112. #280 – Vampires.
113. #287 – A cure is being researched for vampirism.
114. #289 – Their mission is to assassinate the king.
115. #292 – Demons are walking among us.
116. #297 – A woman has adopted Lucifer's child.
117. #301 – "Have you come for my soul?"
118. #302 – Your guardian angel hates you.

119. #308 – Infamous.
120. #310 – You've taken an internship as an evil sidekick.
121. #317 – A retired villain now serving as an advisor to heroes.
122. #319 – Evil lair.
123. #321 – Every villain is a hero in their own mind.
124. #323 – "I'd always wanted to be a hero … Funny how the world works."
125. #327 – A villain's costume.
126. #330 – "Who's ready to get in a little trouble?"
127. #333 – "The hero life's never done anything for me."
128. #338 – Extension.
129. #340 – Fleece.
130. #345 – Burp.
131. #349 – Steps.
132. #352 – Plush.
133. #356 – Box.
134. #358 – Curtain.
135. #360 – Number.
136. #361 – Stage.
137. #362 – Show.
138. #365 – Board.

Supernatural (S)

1. #1 – You've discovered a long lost relative.
2. #2 – You run into yourself in a dream, but something isn't right – they're trying their hardest to stay away from you.
3. #9 – You've been hired as a private investigator.
4. #14 – "Don't you dare."
5. #16 – You're a pirate preparing to set sail.
6. #17 -There's a ghost living in your attic.
7. #24 – A loved one is brought back to life – for a price.
8. #27 – You just discovered you've got extraordinary powers.
9. #28 – You're being hunted down.
10. #29 – You're one of the last humans to survive.
11. #38 – "We don't have time for this!"
12. #42 – The only way to save the future, is to destroy the past.
13. #48 – Your spell will only last for two minutes.
14. #50 – "Good timing."

15. #51 – If you had the ability to see your future, would you?
16. #53 – The ability to stop time.
17. #55 – You're immortal.
18. #58 – Everything's happening in slow motion.
19. #60 – You're face to face with Father Time.
20. #61 – Cats with opposable thumbs.
21. #62 – The ability to speak to and understand animals.
22. #63 – You are a crossbreed between a human and a mystical creature.
23. #64 – Flying monkeys!
24. #69 – "Yeah, when pigs fly."
25. #71 – You've just gotten a dog – only, it's not a dog.
26. #74 – An animal that can speak English.
27. #75 – You've been transformed into an animal.
28. #76 – You've found out your lover is a shapeshifter.
29. #78 – "Get that thing out of here!"
30. #81 – An animal has come back from extinction.
31. #89 – The spirit of a lost pet lingers around your house.
32. #91 – You find a wild horse nursing a unicorn.
33. #93 – Your car has taken over and is taking you somewhere.
34. #107 – Humans have created a serum for immortality.
35. #115 – "Technology is great when it decides to work."
36. #117 – "Dammit! Why won't this stupid thing work?!"
37. #119 – "We didn't have this back in my day."
38. #122 – Area 51 is nothing like you expected.
39. #127 – You're on an alien planet – with no way to get back home.
40. #128 – "How can they be in two places at once?"
41. #134 – This place feels totally different at night.
42. #136 – Go to your happy place. They won't find you there.
43. #138 – You're at the wrong place at the wrong time.
44. #140 – Someone offers to take you to a magical place. Will you go?
45. #145 – "Meet me in the lobby in 10 minutes."
46. #147 – So this is what heaven look like.
47. #148 – So this is what hell looks like.
48. #151 – You never thought you'd be on the other side of a prison cell.
49. #154 – Something's growing in your boss' lab.
50. #158 – The internet is now at your fingertips – literally.

51. #163 – Your scientific experiment is about to go horribly, horribly wrong.
52. #165 – Aliens have agreed to share their scientific knowledge with us.
53. #172 – "There appears to be a chemical reaction happening …"
54. #176 – "We've done it! We've found the cure!"
55. #180 – "This defies everything we know of space and time."
56. #183 – "Tell Dr. Garner I'll be with him in a moment."
57. #189 – Relief.
58. #191 – Joy.
59. #194 – Relaxed.
60. #199 – Lust.
61. #201 – Nostalgia.
62. #204 – Worry.
63. #209 – Determined.
64. #214 – Satisfied.
65. #217 – "This is delicious!"
66. #219 – You have an apprenticeship with your favorite chef.
67. #224 – It's fondue night!
68. #229 – You've burnt it – again.
69. #232 – You find a child going through your trash for food.
70. #239 – You're on the search for a rare fruit in the amazon.
71. #243 – You're so full you could pop.
72. #245 – You've just discovered your great grandfather was a necromancer.
73. #246 – When dusting off an old bottle in the attic, a genie emerges.
74. #248 – Your fiancé has been cursed.
75. #250 – You're trying to learn some magic tricks.
76. #254 – What happens when you accidently cast a curse?
77. #257 – You've been turned into a phoenix.
78. #258 – You're on the verge of creating a new magic system.
79. #259 – A camera that creates 2D clones.
80. #261 – You are a master of the dark arts.
81. #262 – You cast the wrong spell and all hell breaks loose – literally.
82. #264 – Teacher by day, witch hunter by night.
83. #266 – A conversation with your reflection.
84. #268 – "The book of forbidden spells … it's gone missing."
85. #269 – The ability to control shadows.

86. #271 – The ability to manipulate the elements.
87. #272 – "Do you think we could get them to write that scroll for us?"
88. #275 – You've been chosen to be your magic art school's successor.
89. #276 – A werewolf has been reported lurking just outside your town.
90. #278 – You spot a mermaid while out fishing.
91. #279 – After a hard hit to the head, you're starting to see supernatural creatures everywhere you look.
92. #281 – A device that allows you to read people's minds.
93. #284 – The zombie apocalypse has begun.
94. #286 – Something is lurking in the shadows.
95. #288 – Each zodiac sign is granted a set range of abilities.
96. #290 – Mermaids are learning to live on land.
97. #291 – Humans are being harvested to produce blood for vampires.
98. #294 – Humans have become nocturnal.
99. #295 – The afterlife has a receptionist.
100. #297 – A woman has adopted Lucifer's child.
101. #298 – The ability to erase memories.
102. #299 – The full moon's light is acidic.
103. #300 – A cure is being researched for zombies.
104. #302 – Your guardian angel hates you.
105. #305 – You can have any wish granted – for a price.
106. #306 – "Impossible!"
107. #307 – Evil henchmen.
108. #310 – You've taken an internship as an evil sidekick.
109. #314 – Your best friend has decided to join the bad guys.
110. #316 – Rotten to the core.
111. #319 – Evil lair.
112. #321 – Every villain is a hero in their own mind.
113. #324 – You've fallen for the villain.
114. #327 – A villain's costume.
115. #330 – "Who's ready to get in a little trouble?"
116. #331 – Someone thought to be a villain is actually the hero.
117. #334 – A villain driven by logic.
118. #338 – Extension.
119. #343 – Void.
120. #345 – Burp.

121. #349 – Steps.
122. #351 – Frame.
123. #354 – Gold.
124. #362 – Show.

Writing Exercises

1. Create three characters based on three of your favorite colors.
2. Write about a new-found love with someone.
3. Write about someone being betrayed by their best friend.
4. Create a character based on what you had for breakfast.
5. Write about a fight between two people.
6. Write about meeting someone for the first time.
7. Write about someone who is running late for something.
8. Write about someone who is tired of waiting.
9. Write about a world with 30 hours in the day.
10. Write about someone who wants to make up for lost time.
11. Write about someone who is a stickler for being on time.
12. Write about someone who is out of time.
13. Write about the adventures of a lost pet.
14. Write about the world through the perspective of an animal.
15. Write about finding and taking in a baby animal.
16. Write about someone living in the wild.
17. Write a short essay about your favorite animal.
18. Write about what it would be like if dinosaurs were alive today.
19. Write about the first time you got a cellphone.
20. Write about a piece of technology you want to learn how to use.
21. Write about what you would do with a humanoid robot.
22. Write about what you would do if you found a piece of alien technology.
23. What would you invent if you were an inventor?
24. What would happen if all technology suddenly stopped working?
25. What if a new continent was discovered?
26. Write about your spaceship traveling through a black hole.
27. Write about finding a lost child.
28. Write about being teleported.
29. Write about heading off on an adventure at sea.
30. Write about coming home from a long trip.
31. Write about volunteering for an experiment.
32. Write about doing research to find a cure.
33. Write about the process to bring someone or something back to life.
34. Write about finding ancient technology.

35. Write about a device that is threatening humanity.
36. Write about scientists trying to understand magic.
37. Write about someone discovering love for the first time.
38. Write about someone expressing rage.
39. Write about someone showing loyalty.
40. Write about someone being scared.
41. Write about someone working their way through three different emotions.
42. Write about someone causing an emotion in someone else.
43. Write about opening your own restaurant.
44. Write about being poisoned.
45. Write about going apple picking on a date.
46. Write about cooking your favorite meal.
47. Write about going grocery shopping.
48. Write about finding moldy food in your fridge.
49. Creation a recipe for a potion.
50. Write about a witch on the run.
51. Write about a magic student's first day of class.
52. Write about being cursed.
53. Write about fighting an evil warlock.
54. Write about shopping for a wand.
55. Write about your powers being too strong for you to control.
56. Write about the process of becoming a vampire.
57. Write about the process of becoming a werewolf.
58. Write about the process of becoming a zombie.
59. Write about traveling to the afterlife.
60. Write about someone mastering their superpowers.
61. Write about someone losing their superpowers.
62. Write about a villain coming up with a plan.
63. Write about the application process of an evil henchmen.
64. Write about your life as a villain.
65. Write about your life as a hero.
66. Write about the life of a villain's child.
67. Write about a hero who is becoming a villain.
68. Write a scene based around your favorite word.
69. Create three words out of your first and last name, then write a scene using them.
70. Write a scene based on your least favorite word.

71. Pick three words that describe your life, then write a scene based on them.
72. Take the first and last word of your favorite book, then write a scene using them.
73. Take the first and last word of your favorite song, then write a scene using them.

Thank You!

That's all for now! We hope you had fun exploring your creative side! If you did, please considering leaving us a review. We'd really appreciate it!

You can come back next year for our 2021 edition and do a whole new set of prompts, and a new set of exercises.

But in the meantime, if you're looking for something to keep you busy, you can try our other prompt books:

- 365 Drawing Prompts.
- 100 Character Prompts.
- 100 Quote Prompts.
- And more!

And if you're looking for something fun to read to give you some inspiration, check out our fiction books and comics!

For more information, check out our website, www.TCStudiosHQ.com.